NEIL HUMPHREYS

Be My Baby

on the road to fatherhood

mc **Marshall Cavendish**
Editions

Copyright © 2009 Marshall Cavendish International (Asia) Private Limited

Cover and illustrations by Lock Hong Liang

Published by Marshall Cavendish Editions
An imprint of Marshall Cavendish International
1 New Industrial Road, Singapore 536196

Other Marshall Cavendish Offices
Marshall Cavendish Ltd. 5th Floor, 32–38 Saffron Hill, London EC1N 8FH, UK • Marshall Cavendish Corporation. 99 White Plains Road, Tarrytown NY 10591-9001, USA • Marshall Cavendish International (Thailand) Co Ltd. 253 Asoke, 12th Flr, Sukhumvit 21 Road, Klongtoey Nua, Wattana, Bangkok 10110, Thailand • Marshall Cavendish (Malaysia) Sdn Bhd, Times Subang, Lot 46, Subang Hi-Tech Industrial Park, Batu Tiga, 40000 Shah Alam, Selangor Darul Ehsan, Malaysia

Marshall Cavendish is a trademark of Times Publishing Limited

National Library Board Singapore Cataloguing in Publication Data
Humphreys, Neil.
Be my baby / Neil Humphreys. – Singapore : Marshall Cavendish Editions, c2009.
p. cm.

ISBN-13 : 978-981-261-658-6

1. Fatherhood – Humor.   2. Pregnancy – Humor.   3. Humphreys, Neil – Humor.

I. Title.

HQ756

306.87420207 – dc22   OCN255864329

Printed in Singapore by Times Graphics Pte Ltd

Contents

Acknowledgements

Just a couple of days after hearing the good news, my mother called and suggested that the road to fatherhood had the makings of a book. With a hollow laugh, I dismissed the idea as impractical. I was about to become a first-time father, for heaven's sake. Where would I find the time?

Several months later, I called my mum to inform her that the book was almost finished and to thank her for such an ingenious idea. I still don't know where I found the time.

I am also indebted to Chris and the rest of the gang at Marshall Cavendish International (Asia) for being so loyal and supportive. Mei Lin sent adorably polite emails telling me to hurry up and Hong Liang produced a wonderfully zany cover while Katharine was always on hand to rein in the self-indulgence and minimise the swearing.

This journey began with one mother's idea and finished with another's bravery. This book could not have been written without its inspirational central character. My heroic wife agreed to let me follow her around for almost nine months with a notepad while asking daft questions like "So how many times did you pee last night, mate? Was it six or seven?"

Thanks, Tracy, for just about everything really.

for the little heifer ...

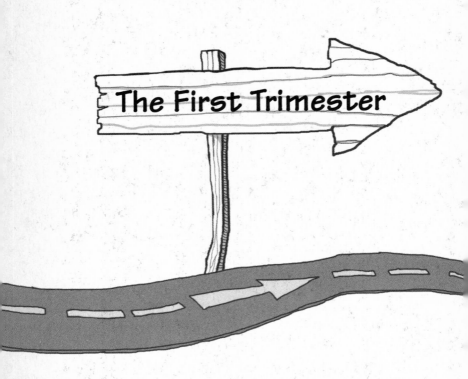

The First Trimester

Friday, 5 October 2007

Two lines. There they were. Two lines. Oh shit. Two lines. Surely, it was a dream sequence. Two lines. I was treading water in slow motion. The bathroom took on surrealist qualities. True, I had just watched my wife pee on a plastic contraption but that only added to the slightly out-of-body experience. I had never watched my wife urinate on a plastic contraption before, but then it would prove to be a day of firsts.

A moment earlier, she had passed me the oval-shaped, white plastic contraption. It reminded me of a fried egg—a fried egg that someone had just peed on.

"Lay it flat on the top of the toilet," my toilet-bound wife ordered.

"Why have I got to take it? It's covered in piss," I replied petulantly, clearly taking the shine off the potentially beautiful moment for my wife.

"It's got to be left face up and flat to get a more accurate reading," said the lady on the throne.

With a theatrical sigh, I took the still warm plastic contraption, held it at arm's length in such a way that it suggested it was radioactive and rested it on top of the toilet. I love my wife dearly, but there is a line. Well, actually, there were two lines. I noticed them almost instantly. My facial expression at this sudden development clearly betrayed me because my wife began jigging up and down on the toilet and shouting, "What? What is it? What have you seen? What does it say? You've looked at it before me, haven't you? I told you not to do that. Well, what does it say then?"

She often does this. Argue with herself and win.

"Er, I saw something but I genuinely don't know what it means."

Sad but true. She had read the instructions before taking aim. I hadn't.

"Well, what does it say?" my excited wife cried, craning her head left and right and waddling slightly from side to side like a disoriented penguin. "I can't see it."

"Two lines have come up," I replied with all the casualness of a man who hasn't read the instructions.

"In which window?"

"What do you mean which window?"

"Is it in the square window or the round window? Are the lines in the same window or is there one in the square window and one in the round?"

"Round windows? Square windows? What is this? Bloody *Play School*?"

"Don't mess about. Give it to me."

For the second time in two minutes, I handled a urine-stained plastic contraption, lifting it from the back of the toilet. My indomitable wife snatched it from my tentative grasp and stared at it for several seconds. Then she smiled. Now, I know she was sitting on a toilet with most of her clothes around her ankles and holding something that now had a distinct whiff of piss, but she had never looked more beautiful.

"Neil, I'm pregnant," she said softly.

And we both burst out laughing.

That was when the surrealism kicked in. It was not real. Or at least, it didn't seem real. I had waited for this moment, rehearsed this moment, for years. I met my wife fifteen years ago. I've known her half my life. When she came down the stairs of our Year 12 common room and offered me some of her strawberry lip balm, I had a vague idea that we'd probably end up being in this situation at some point in our lives. Perhaps not fifteen years later. Having grown up in Dagenham, on a Greater London council estate, some of my peers ended up in this situation fifteen minutes later. I had anticipated this moment for several years because I'm sentimental. That's why we still have that almost-empty Body Shop jar of strawberry lip balm in the house. And it smells worse than the plastic contraption that my wife was holding in her hands.

She was pregnant. My wife was pregnant. She was not going to have a baby though. Don't be ridiculous. She was just pregnant. That was all. I could not connect the dots. There was a chemical malfunction in my brain and it was refusing to compute. I'd waited for this moment for fifteen years and now that it was here, it was literally too mind-blowing to digest. Instead it played with me; it toyed with me. We giggled like cheeky cherubs and danced around the bathroom to Judy Garland—once my wife had pulled up her trousers.

The recriminations followed the dancing.

"I told you I was pregnant, didn't I?" my wife said, after slumping onto the sofa to rub her belly for the first time. My God, it would not be the last.

"Yeah, you did."

"I can't believe you forced me to paint the fence last weekend."

My wife often speaks in such absolute, melodramatic tones, intimating that I had held a gun to her temple and screamed, "Paint the fence, woman, or I'll blow your head off."

"How was I to know you were pregnant? Besides, I only asked you to help with the paint touch-ups. It's not like I had you up a ladder with a roller."

"Well, I knew I was pregnant. I just had a feeling."

"And missing your period was a fairly big clue, I suppose?"

"All right, smart arse, but I did tell you I was pregnant."

She had. But I was sceptical. Even the two lines were not yet conclusive proof. I need a weatherman to tell me when it's raining.

"I'm not being all doom and gloom but we've waited a long time for this and I want everything to be confirmed first. I want to make sure that everything is perfect," insisted my tedious voice of reason.

It's true. I did. Throughout the pregnancy, I wanted everything to be as perfect as possible. On the road to fatherhood, I turned into Mary Poppins.

"You're such a miserable sod sometimes," my wife pointed out.

"You know these pregnancy tests are not foolproof. Let's take another one tomorrow and then we can be totally sure and see the doctor."

"All right, but I'm not going through all that supermarket nonsense again."

Saturday, 6 October

I admit that I did behave like a nervous schoolboy sneaking a "crafty fag" behind the bike sheds yesterday. I was only buying a pregnancy test kit but you would have thought that I was surreptitiously picking up some gear from a crack den. Checking over both shoulders, I skulked down the aisles for several minutes, taking a disturbing level of interest in underarm deodorant, while waiting for an elderly man to make a final decision on the colour of a toothbrush. Finally satisfied that the middle-aged chap further down the aisle was distracted by a three-blade razor special offer, I swooped.

There was more than one option. Suddenly, I was eighteen and buying condoms all over again. I hadn't bought condoms for ages. Obviously. In fact, long ago I vowed to never buy them again; there were too many colours, options, sizes and materials to choose from. Condoms present more choices than just about any other item found in a supermarket aisle even though everyone knows that most teenage boys would remove a testicle with a three-blade razor before asking an employee for advice. To alleviate my embarrassment, I always picked the pack of three closest to hand and usually went home equipped with a contraceptive device fit for a woolly mammoth. Images of those winter Olympians who slip out of their toboggans often came to mind at the most unfortunate of moments.

And here I was, stuck in the same aisle. It was interesting to note that the various pregnancy test kits were beside the extensive condom collection. If you forgot one, at least you knew where to find the other.

"Which one shall we get?" I hissed at my wife.

"Ooh, I don't know. This one's cheaper but this one claims to have a guaranteed accuracy reading," she replied, holding the kits aloft like a militant protestor.

"Here, put your hands down. What are you doing? I don't want people to see what we're doing."

"Bloody hell, Neil, you're 32."

I am, but that doesn't do anything for the chip on the shoulder. I come from Dagenham, England. Until the 1960s, Dagenham could proudly claim to be home to the largest council estate in the world. It now boasts one of the highest teenage pregnancy rates in Europe. A few of my old schoolmates had contributed to the statistics by the time they were seventeen, one or two had to miss the odd final exam to give birth, which must have played havoc with their revision schedule. A very close friend went a step further by getting his best mate's girlfriend pregnant when she was sixteen and while his best mate was at football training. He scored with his boots off and I heard his best mate had a stinker in training, too. Dagenham has produced Dudley Moore, Sir Alf Ramsey, Terry Venables, Jimmy Greaves and Sandie Shaw because it has never stopped bloody producing. I have always felt that it's my socio-economic duty to get someone pregnant in the back of an old Ford.

The misguided, not to mention obsessive, paranoia remains. Am I old enough to be a father? Am I old enough? Have I distanced myself enough from my teens to avoid slipping into a cliché?

Bloody hell, Neil, you're 32.

"Right, we're having this one," I declared.

"Why?"

"Because it says it's got a good accuracy reading."

"And it's the cheapest?"

"That too."

We came. We saw. My wife peed on a stick. But it wasn't enough. I needed foolproof evidence, confirmation that the first test was not a fluke, that somehow the human chorionic gonadotropin, the peptide hormone produced in pregnancy (I looked it up), was not giving us a false reading. Even when it comes to the creation of life, I want a second opinion. I'm very anal that way.

So we embarked on a second trip to a different supermarket (just in case the first supermarket sold defective home pregnancy kits, you understand) in a different town (just in case the first town sold, well, you know). Fortunately, we had gone away for the weekend. We live in the Australian seaside town of Geelong in Victoria and had recently booked a trip to the historic gold-mining town of Bendigo, about an hour from Melbourne. Of course, we had booked the weekend for two, having no idea that three of us might end up making the trip. After the positive reading, we still decided to take the three-hour journey. We considered it to be our first break as a family. We can be very soppy at times.

My wife had reservations about the mine though. We'd booked an underground tour of Bendigo's Central Deborah Gold Mine. The town's last commercial mine, it unearthed almost one tonne of gold from 1939 to 1954 and remains one of Victoria's most popular tourist attractions. The only drawback was that my wife was concerned she might go into labour down there, less than 24 hours after passing a pregnancy test.

"Do you think we should really go down this mine?" she asked, while perusing the attraction's leaflet. "It says here that we're going to be at least twenty storeys underground."

"We'll be all right. There will be a guide in there with us."

"What if something happens to the baby?"

"In less than 24 hours? You're not going to give birth down there."

"No, I mean the mine itself. I'm worried about too much physical exertion. I've got to make sure I don't overdo it."

"It's only a tour of the mine. They are not going to give you a miner's helmet and a pickaxe and ask you to dig for your dinner, are they?"

"Well, I've got to take it easy now that I'm pregnant."

This was the first time that my wife officially acknowledged she was pregnant in an almost matter-of-fact fashion. It made me smile.

The supermarket trip was less of an ordeal the second time around. The prospect of fatherhood had put my obsessive trivialities into perspective. I could be a father less than nine months from now. Someone might look up to me and call me "daddy". I had more pressing priorities than what strangers in a strange supermarket might think of me as I threw a home pregnancy test into a basket. I had acquired a profound sense of maturity in the last 24 hours. I had also acquired a large Toblerone to cover the home pregnancy test with.

The second test was a subdued, routine affair. We both sensed it before going into the unfamiliar bathroom in our caravan park budget cabin; a strange venue to confirm whether or not we were on the way to having our first child. Nevertheless, my wife peed and we both agreed. We were on the path to parenthood. You can't cheat two pregnancy tests; two lines in two tests on two separate days. We still have both pregnancy kits in our bathroom cabinet. That's what the giddy rush of impending fatherhood can do; it makes you keep objects that your wife urinated on beside your shampoo and shower gel. But I didn't care. At that moment, I would have framed them both and hung them beside my limited edition *Star Wars* poster in the living room. I was elated and apprehensive in equal measure. My wife was pregnant. Two pregnancy tests had made it conclusive. It was absolute. Now, I'll just wait for the doctor to confirm it.

Sunday, 7 October

I awoke to the sound of my wife retching. It was an awful wake-up call. My wife is never sick. Never. It's quite extraordinary. She's been a preschool teacher for over ten years now and hasn't missed a single day through illness. She's taught in England, Singapore and now Australia and has never succumbed to the usual coughs, colds and ailments that spread through a kindergarten classroom. I've never known her to vomit or spend hours in bed with a fever. There was an unfortunate incident involving a case of acute diarrhoea and a pair of jeans that forced her to miss most of Frank Bruno's heavyweight title triumph against Oliver McCall in 1995 but that's another story (and another pair of borrowed jeans). When I sneeze, it's an allergy. When I cough, it's a cold and when I come down with a fever, I make my funeral arrangements. I have long admired (and secretly envied) her physical fortitude.

She was crouched over the toilet and in obvious discomfort. I had never seen her like this before. My rock—the woman who once fractured two fingers but didn't realise until hours later when she complained of some soreness—looked vulnerable. I rubbed her back gently. It didn't alleviate the retching, nor check the growing sense of uselessness on my part.

"I'm sorry, mate," my wife grumbled from the toilet bowl.

"Don't be silly. It's all right."

"I woke up feeling really nauseous, stuck my head down the toilet and I've been here ever since."

Rather tentatively, I craned my head over my wife's and peered into the toilet bowl. I was greeted by the horrifying, sickening, traumatising sight of absolutely nothing.

"Er, mate. There's nothing in the toilet," I ventured cautiously. I didn't want my retching wife to suddenly spin around and turn into the exorcist.

"I know. That's the thing. I can't seem to bring anything up. I keep retching but nothing's coming out."

She retched again, quite violently, but she was right. There was no vomit. She spat a few times to clear her mouth.

"So it's not morning sickness as such," I pondered aloud, which was not the smartest move. "It's really like, well, spitting with aggression."

My wife froze momentarily before turning her head slowly to look up at me. She did look remarkably like Linda Blair at that moment.

"Neil, why don't you piss off?"

So I did. I retreated to the bedroom and then remembered my manners.

"Can I get you anything or do anything for you, mate?"

"Yeah, you can piss off."

In my defence, I don't know anything. Really. It's not an "ah shucks", cutesy, cutesy act to gain sympathy. I really don't know anything about pregnancy. I have been dropped onto the path to parenthood but I don't know the way. Haven't got a clue. My ignorance when it comes to doing the most natural thing my species does is quite extraordinary. I've written a few books and interviewed prime ministers, rock stars, Oscar-winning actors and even David Beckham (I slipped that one in because if you Google his name in the years to come, this book title might pop up), but when it comes to procreation, embryos, ovaries, foetus growth and baby behaviour, I know next to nothing. My sister, who gave birth to three boys within two years (she had twins; she's not in any science journals), is occasionally tickled, and frequently disturbed, when her big brother's childlike innocence threatens to cause serious injury.

Take, for instance, the time I sat her two-month-old firstborn upright on the sofa and got up to turn on the TV while he lurched, not unimpressively, to his left and slid down the sofa like a drunk on a park bench. Or the time I held him in my arms and watched as his head flopped backwards over my elbow and asked, in all seriousness, "Why doesn't he just lift his head up?"

And then there are the daft, inappropriate questions: Can he have some of my doughnut? How about a nice slice of crusty bread? When breastfeeding, do you always use the same breast? Now that you've got twins, do you use both breasts at the same time like a sow in a sty? Aren't babies cute when they're running around with their little bottoms out? At what age am I supposed to stop saying that?

I am rather proud of my childlike curiosity. But like a child, I should be seen and not heard when I'm in the presence of parents and toddlers, according to my wife. We now have a policy that all baby questions must be vetted by her before she decides if they are socially or intellectually appropriate. Most of them are not and I'm genuinely concerned about my sudden, uncensored remarks and exclamations at future doctor's appointments and antenatal classes. Curiosity, and an appalling sense of timing, will be my downfall.

A couple of years ago in Singapore, my wife and I bumped into a former colleague in a shopping mall. Without thinking, I asked, "Hey, how are you? Not long now, eh? So when's the baby due?"

"I gave birth a month ago," she replied.

What can you say to that? There is no suitable response in that situation; no reply can save a faux pas of that magnitude. I could not blame it on a miscalculation of the dates or the fact that our paths hadn't crossed for a few weeks or even attribute it to characteristic absent-mindedness. I was suggesting she was fat, and her extraordinarily muscular husband knew it.

"Why the hell did you say that?" my wife demanded, the moment she dragged my red face away.

"I don't know. I thought it would be a nice thing to say."

"Nice? You told her she was fat. You can tell she's not pregnant anymore. Her belly shape's completely different. She doesn't have a big bulge around her belly button. She's walking normally. She didn't seem out of breath. There's a million ways you could tell she wasn't pregnant."

And I had failed to spot them all. I still would and it's my turn now. We're having a baby. I've got less than nine months to ask as many stupid questions as I can.

Monday, 8 October

We have booked an appointment to see our local doctor to confirm, confirm and confirm that we really are having a baby. The receptionist clearly detected our sense of urgency down the line. She pencilled us in for next Monday when the doctor returns from his holiday. We have got to play the old waiting game.

The suspense will drive my wife crazy. She cannot read an Agatha Christie novel without reading the back page first, so by the seventh day I expect her to be tapping on the doctor's surgery door with a bottle of urine. She hasn't vomited yet. The aggressive spitting has subsided too, thankfully.

Wednesday, 10 October

My wife has just called and suggested that we speak to the doctor's receptionist again to ask if there has been a cancellation. She wants to move the appointment forward. The suspense has taken its toll. She lasted two days.

Friday, 12 October

Five weeks today. The embryo is reaching the size of a tip of a pen. These are my wife's calculations so I'll take her at her word for now. Besides, she's only just started talking to me again after

I failed to get the doctor's appointment moved forward.

If the embryo is now five weeks old, then its heart will begin to beat at the end of next week. That's surreal, as is my constant humming of "Two Hearts" by Phil Collins. The last time I sang a Phil Collins song was some time around 1987 and it was most likely "Against All Odds", probably because I was desperate to get off with Kelly Stewart, the best-looking girl in Dagenham. There was more chance of me getting off with Phil Collins.

Interestingly, it was around that time that my now pregnant wife subconsciously saw the future father of her child for the first time. From the legendary Mayesbrook Comprehensive School's Music Club, I was selected to perform Elvis's "Love Me Tender" to the whole school on the grounds that I owned my own keyboard. It was a Christmas present that I'd wanted because you could do basic sampling by recording a sound and playing it back on the keys. When you're twelve, you can have endless fun recording the word "bollocks" and hearing it continuously in different pitches as you run your fingers along the keyboard. How was I to know that that keyboard would unlock my musical prowess and allow me to master "Love Me Tender" and "Axel F" within six months of each other? On the raised stage of the school assembly hall, I stood alongside five other fellow keyboard owners as the pop drumbeat on the music teacher's synthesizer counted us in and off we went on our musical journey. And as one-handed keyboard playing goes, we were spectacularly ordinary.

More than ten years later, my wife and I were sitting in our apartment in Singapore when she told me about her cousin being in our school band.

"Yeah, he played keyboards or something," she recalled. "I remember one year, we came into assembly to watch his year play some Elvis song."

"'Love Me Tender'!"

"Yeah, that was it."

"That was me, too! I was on stage. Do you remember me? I stood right next to your cousin. Didn't I stand out or anything?"

"No, not at all," replied the future carrier of my embryo. "I thought you were all shit."

Sunday, 14 October

We are 24 hours away from our local doctor ending his extended holiday and I feel strangely ambivalent. My wife is pregnant. We are pregnant but we are not having a baby. My mind is still stubbornly refusing to make the connection. I find myself repeating "my wife's pregnant, my wife's pregnant, my wife's pregnant" in a cynical attempt to reach some distant nirvana. Barring an unthinkable disaster at the doctor's surgery, my wife is pregnant. We will have a baby. We have been waiting for this moment for years. From the moment our paths crossed in school for the first time without me playing an Elvis ballad, we kind of knew that we would reach this juncture at some point. I've wanted to become a dad more than I've wanted just about anything else: hair, bigger biceps, the ability to score a hat-trick at Upton Park, a university degree, anything. Now it's about to become a reality but I cannot reach my wife's natural high. I'm walking with a bit of a spring in my step, but she's floating and I want to soar with her.

It's not for the want of trying. Apart from my daft, whispered mantra, I share her enthusiasm in all the baby talk—and since last Friday we have discussed little else—but I can't quite get there. There is a laid-back calmness, a certain serenity even, where unchecked jubilation and hysteria should be. After fifteen years of waiting for the doctor to say "yes", I fear a sense of anticlimax sneaking in and I'm struggling to deal with it. This is not how I'm supposed to feel. Even hinting at the possibility of an anticlimax simply accentuates my guilt and adds to the feeling of anticlimax. While my wife climbs the ceiling, I'm being the voice of reason. Let's not get excited until we get the doctor's confirmation. Let's not get carried away until we reach the end of the first trimester. We can't tell anyone until we are way past the twelve-week mark and have cleared all the relevant health hurdles at that stage. I want to be Mr Fun Dad. I sound like Oscar the Grouch in *Sesame Street*.

Part of the problem is that nothing has changed, superficially at least. I'm not pregnant. My wife is, but she doesn't look any different and, apart from that spitting incident in the Bendigo cabin, hasn't behaved any differently. Nothing has changed, but everything has changed and I should be acting accordingly. The truth is that there's nothing to do and I can't shake off this permeating sense of ambivalence. Ironically, I've never felt more impotent and it's extremely disconcerting. If necessary, I will whisper my mantra all the way into the doctor's office. My wife is pregnant, my wife is pregnant, my wife is pregnant …

Monday, 15 October

The doctor did not even have the merest hint of a tan after returning from his holiday. These medicos really are sun smart, aren't they? Those were my first, ridiculous thoughts when I sat down beside his desk. Flippant, I know, but I was both optimistically expectant and nervous; a strange combination of anxiety and quiet confidence that I hadn't felt since I took my final university exams. Sitting beside the doctor's desk while he finished off some two-finger typing on his laptop was like being sent to the headmaster's office at the end of term to show off my best artwork. Well, sir, look at the masterpiece that I've produced this time.

His two-finger typing was shockingly slow for a man who conducted basic medical procedures with his hands. Just two weeks earlier, those hands had thrust a metallic syringe into my ears to flush out all the blocked wax. I expected those hands to be more proficient when he started poking and prodding around my wife's pelvis in the weeks to come.

A lifetime passed before he finally looked up from what I hope wasn't an email to his wife telling her what he wanted for dinner and said, "Hello again. I see all the blood tests gave us the results we were looking for."

Almost a month earlier, we had told our jet-setting physician that we planned to start a family. So he sent my wife for a few routine blood tests to confirm that she was capable of bearing children. Three weeks later and here we were. If I may strut my masculinity for a moment and go all alpha-male, I don't mess about, you know.

"So it looks like you're ready to make a baby," the doctor said, smiling only at my wife I might add. "What can I do for you today?"

"We think we've made a baby already," I interjected, re-establishing my status as the dominant ape in foreign territory. If I were a dog, I might have peed on his desk.

"Really? That was quick, wasn't it?" he said, this time smiling at me.

Better believe it, baby.

"We took a couple of tests and they were both positive," said my wife, as I struggled to resist the temptation to strut around the doctor's surgery singing "I've got a lovely bunch of coconuts".

"So we're hoping you would confirm it for us."

"Well, it sounds to me like you've confirmed it already. Those tests are little different to the ones we have here but, for peace of mind, we'll do another one if you like."

He led my wife out into the corridor and left me alone in his office. There was a plastic model of a female pelvis on his desk. I picked it up. No baby of mine is going to fit through that, I thought. The door suddenly opened and, in blind panic, I nearly threw the plastic pelvis up in the air. Thankfully, it was not the doctor but my wife holding a plastic bowl.

"Where's the doctor?" she whispered.

"I don't know, mate. I thought he was with you."

My wife left the room again. She returned seconds later, still holding the plastic bowl.

"Well, he's not out in the corridor," she said. "What do you think I should do with this?"

"What is it?"

"It's my urine. He told me to fill the bowl and give it to one of the nurses but there's no one out there."

"Can't you take it out to one of the girls on the front desk?" I suggested.

"It's a bowl of piss, Neil," replied my wife. "I can't wander around the patients out in reception carrying this, can I?"

"Yeah, but you can't sit in here with it either."

"I'm going back into the corridor. You're useless, you are."

She often goes into Yoda-speak when she's telling me off. I was left alone once more. I was beginning to think that I spent more time in the doctor's office than the doctor. After fiddling with the plastic pelvis for a few more minutes, I was eventually rejoined by my flustered, but smiling, wife.

"It's all right," she said. "I found a nurse who said she'd give it to the doctor when she found him."

"Found him? Has he got lost?"

"Just shut up and wait."

I spent several, entertaining minutes demonstrating to my wife, via the plastic pelvis, the kind of margins she'd be dealing with in the delivery room. She looked horrified.

After what must have been an extended lunch break followed by a trip to the betting shop, the doctor finally returned holding a plastic pregnancy contraption.

"You are going to have a baby, aren't you?"

Even the eternal pessimist in the room couldn't argue with three positive tests. We were definitely on our way now. The man in the white coat had confirmed it.

"So what do we do now?" I asked the doctor.

He smiled as he went back to his two-finger typing.

"No, really, doctor. What do we do now?"

For those parents who think I'm veering towards the melodramatic, consider this baby-making checklist: Did you give birth in a foreign country? Had you lived in that country for less than two years? Were you without healthcare cover in that country? Were you the only ones living in the country, with no family members or close friends around to assist with the birth and offer any pearls of pregnancy wisdom?

If you answered "yes" to all of the above questions, then a) welcome to our world and b) how the hell did you do it?

Even the doctor stopped his two-finger typing for a moment and looked up when I told him that we were alone in Australia—no other family or friends—and that the reciprocal health agreement between Australia and Britain did not apply to us because we had not been resident in Britain for the past five years. From 1996 to 2006, we had lived in Singapore, where we had a great time and I wrote some books about the marvellous country. Book royalties might contribute to the odd crib and carrycot, but they sure ain't no Medicare card.

I'm not looking for a string quartet to play a sad song for me here. My parents divorced when I was four and, for many years, we never had, to quote my mother, "a pot to piss in". I've interviewed young mothers cradling their newborns while living in tents in post-tsunami Aceh. So perspective has never been a problem. It's just that as a prospective father, I'm determined to make sure that my wife doesn't miss out on anything critical to our baby's development. If she needs to take a tablespoon of crude oil three times a day, I want to know about it and I'll make damn sure that she gets it.

"Is there anything she shouldn't do?" I persisted while the doctor's increasing typing speed suggested he was eager to move on to his next patient.

"Well, hang-gliding is probably out of the question."

He was a comedian.

"Just maintain a regular diet, avoid saunas or anything else that could make you too hot and stay away from old cheese."

Oh, the double entendres I could have made there, but I'm about to become a father, you know.

My wife could also look forward to having sore and tender breasts and nausea from around the six- to the sixteen-week period. I could look forward to my wife having sore and tender breasts and a period of nausea from around the six- to the sixteen-week period. We could hardly wait.

Wednesday, 17 October

We were officially on our way to making another human being so we sat down to discuss *that* pregnancy dilemma. You know the one. At this stage, it's the only one—when do we go public?

The excitable, perennial optimist struggled to contain her joy the moment two lines popped up in the correct window. The hard-headed, dispiriting pessimist wanted to wait until he was certain there could be no further complications. Say, in about eight or nine months from now.

Not that we anticipated any problems in going public. On the contrary, our parents have been hanging on our every word for several years now in anticipation that the word "pregnancy" might crop up in conversation. You have no idea the number of anticlimactic moments our parents have experienced lately. My mother-in-law is convinced that every postcard, birthday present or Christmas gift she receives is going to be a photocopy of our baby's first ultrasound scan. How do you compete with that? Imagine her disappointment when she opens the parcel and discovers it really is only a koala fridge magnet. My father-in-law is just brusque.

My wife speaks to her parents every week via an online messenger service. The topic of pregnancy is always painfully short.

"Are you pregnant yet?" my father-in-law will ask his daughter.

"No, dad."

"Bloody useless, he is."

Notice that I am clearly the defective component in the baby-making process. It's never his beloved daughter. She is the cute one, the cuddly one, the apple of his jaundiced eye. No, it must be that lanky husband firing more blanks than the Territorial Army.

"Are you sure you're not pregnant yet?" my father-in-law will continue, as if my wife could unknowingly be pregnant but had put the nausea and the swollen stomach down to an undercooked paneer makhani.

"No, dad. When we are, we will tell you, I promise."

"He's a right wanker, that Neil."

I've been a "right wanker", in the benign, affectionate, son-in-law sense, since I married his daughter and failed to produce a grandchild within nine months of our wedding day. Clearly I was not doing something right and "needed a bit more bloody practice" to quote him verbatim. Paradoxically, I was also a "right wanker" before our wedding day precisely because I fancied the idea of getting a bit more practice. I couldn't win.

Before we moved to Singapore, I used to sleep on my future in-laws' sofa every Saturday night, desperately hoping to get a bit more practice but it just never happened. My future father-in-law had obviously loosened the hinge on the living room door because whenever his daughter opened it, the door creaked like a bad prop in a Roger Corman movie. Doing my best Boris Karloff, I would sit bolt upright on the sofa as he shouted, "Get back up to bed now. You can see Neil in the morning."

Less than five hours later, he would come into the living room, climb onto the sofa and plant both knees into my groin, which made me jump up and smother him like a Venus flytrap.

"Oh, sorry, Neil," he'd say in mock innocence while leaning over to the curtains. "I'm just opening the curtains. Did I wake you?"

"No, not at all," I would groan.

"You sound terrible. Did you drink too much last night?"

"No, it's not that. You're kneeling on my testicles."

Before our wedding, one man and his dressing gown stood between us getting a bit of practice. After we exchanged vows, my in-laws sent us to our bedroom to think about what we hadn't done. We were not allowed out until we had something to show for our efforts.

My mum, on the other hand, loves subtle. She refuses to play banal mind games; she invents them. Unlike my in-laws, she has never asked the question directly. Opting for nuanced diplomacy, she skirts around the fringes like an Olympic skater.

"It's a nice little car, good to get about," she said when she visited recently and climbed into our tiny fuel-efficient vehicle that does its bit for the environment but is little bigger than a kiddy's car. "But it won't be big enough when you have a baby."

"No, probably not. We might have to trade it in when we get pregnant."

"How long do you reckon you'll keep this car?"

When she inspected our home for the first time, she connected interior decorating to producing grandchildren.

"That's a nice room you've got there," she remarked. "Would make a lovely nursery."

"Yeah, we'll turn it into a nursery when we get pregnant."

"When do you think you'll start redecorating?"

My mother eased off for a while when my younger sister suddenly went from nought to three boys in two years. This proved to be a wonderful diversionary tactic. However, my sister's boys are all now tiptoeing towards kindergarten. Once again, we found ourselves out of distractions and the harsh glare of the parental spotlight can be unremitting. The message from our parents has been unequivocal: none of us is getting any younger so stop the clock and give us a grandchild.

All of this underlines the importance of selecting the appropriate date to tell our families. My wife sensibly picked any time past the three-month mark. After the first trimester, most of the baby's structures should be safely in place. I stubbornly persisted with four months to give the foetus a chance to really bed down.

"Bed down?" said my distinctly unimpressed wife. "It's not a bunch of daffodils."

"I know that but I'd just prefer those extra four weeks for peace of mind. You know what I'm like."

We compromised. Twelve weeks would take us into early December, so how about a Christmas Day announcement? My wife wasn't sure she could wait that long but agreed that it would be the perfect present. I'm already dreaming of a Christmas where I won't be called a wanker by my father-in-law.

Friday, 19 October

Six weeks today. The embryonic period has officially kicked off and it is approximately the size of a baked bean.

To honour the occasion, I treated myself to a plate of baked beans on toast. However, I pulled out the tin opener not in Australia, but Singapore.

I found myself cooking alone in a loft apartment overlooking the Singapore River, eight hours away by plane from my wife and our baked bean. Almost a year earlier, I had been invited back to our former home to give a few literature talks at the inaugural Singapore Sun Festival and plug my other books to a new audience. Would I be able to accept a free flight, free accommodation and the odd five-course meal at Raffles Hotel? How could I say no? When we were kids, my sister and I used to wait at the front door because my mother had promised to bring a bag of broken biscuits back from the canteen where she worked.

It all sounded too good to be true. There had to be catch.

The catch arrived in the shape of our baked bean. I seriously contemplated not going. My wife's nausea was due to kick off and I was expected to be in another continent, discussing the merits of a summer home I could never afford in Tuscany with people I didn't know. I felt like a shit and was desperately hoping my partner would hand me a get-out-of-jail free card.

"Of course you have to go," insisted my admirably resilient wife. "I've got loads of class materials and lesson plans to get ready."

"No, I'll stay. I can't leave you on your own. Let me stay."

"No, you want me to tell you to stay, but you know you can't. You've still got to earn some money for me and the baked bean."

She was right. I had to go. I knew that. But it didn't stop me from feeling like a shit.

Monday, 22 October

If I was not convinced before, I am now. I am a shit. My wife called me this morning and I was initially rather abrupt because I was heading out the door to attend a festival event.

"I feel terrible," she croaked down the phone. "So I've taken two days sick leave from work."

I wasn't going anywhere. My wife is never ill. She collected those 100 per cent attendance certificates at the end of every school term with monotonous regularity (in seven years of secondary school, I only earned the attendance certificate once and the teachers gave me a standing ovation) and her work attendance rate was the stuff of legend within Singapore's preschool circles (i.e. my wife and her three colleagues).

"I don't have the energy to get off the sofa," she whispered. "I've completely lost my appetite."

"Really? Not even a chocolate bar?"

"No, I can't stomach chocolate at the moment."

This was serious.

Overwhelmed with fatigue, she had spent most of the time gagging. There was no vomit but a return to that violent spitting, topped off with a nauseous sensation at the back of her throat and the constant taste of soap in her mouth.

Feeling even more redundant than usual, I insisted that she must not move from the sofa for the next 48 hours and extracted a promise that she would call our doctor if any of the symptoms worsened.

"Do you want me to come back?" I asked, already knowing the answer.

"You know you can't. You've got more talks to do."

"Yeah, but I feel shitty now."

"I don't think you feel as bad as me, Neil. Do you?"

She can always slice through my indulgent self-pity. She was right, of course, but that didn't alleviate my persistent guilt. As I'm sure most fathers will readily testify, pregnancy is a painfully one-sided process at this stage (well, at almost every stage from here on in). As the male partner in this lopsided enterprise, you've done your bit, accepted all the backslapping (if you've been brave enough to go public) and nodded in agreement when reference has been made to the potent levels of lead in your pencil. You are a walking advertisement for masculinity "and—which is more—you'll be a Man, my son!" and all that other chest-beating Kipling stuff. Now sit back and watch a bit of football while your partner parks herself in front of the porcelain for the next three months.

As our baked bean grows, so too does the feeling of impotency on my part. Of course, it doesn't help that I'm temporarily housed on another continent in a loft apartment serviced by a middle-aged cleaner who likes to wander in when I'm in various stages of undress. Isolated and useless, the guilt never goes away.

Wednesday, 24 October

There is a lump. Or at least I thought it was a lump. It might have been the result of a plate of lightly buttered toast (which is all my wife can hold down at the moment) but she is positive she has a lump and I am inclined to agree with her.

The image itself was pretty grainy. My wife turned on the webcam in Australia, thrust out her stomach and lifted her shirt slightly so I could just about make out her peanut-sized bump on a laptop in Singapore.

"Are you sure it's a lump?" I asked across cyberspace.

"What else could it be? It's the baby's bump," replied my indignant wife.

"I'm sure it is. It's just that, well …"

"Well, what?"

"Well, I've seen bigger lumps after a curry."

"It's the baby, I'm telling you."

She is determined to get that bump as soon as possible. Before I left, she was jutting out her stomach in the street and demanding to know if her waist size was expanding. When I confirmed that it wasn't, she would sulk before consuming anything her temperamental stomach could keep down.

"You see, look again. I do look bigger now," she insisted, via the webcam.

"Yeah, you do. You look great."

She smiled back at me. A little white lie across two continents never hurt anybody.

After two days on the sofa, she returned to work today feeling marginally more energetic but her condition fluctuates on an hourly basis. To combat the omnipresent nausea, her health programme consists of toast, bananas, folic acid (which helps protect against a number of congenital malformations in the brain and spine) and three naps a day.

I miss her so much.

Friday, 26 October

Seven weeks today. It's a baked bean no more. It is now slightly bigger than a pencil-top eraser but weighs less than an aspirin tablet.

Having been away from my wife and my eraser for over a week now, I felt compelled to do something positive, something fatherly and instructive. The best I could come up with was trawl through Internet sites and chat rooms devoted to expectant fathers and new dads. It was a terrifying experience that I am not eager to repeat.

Men, and I include myself in this, have changed, haven't they? No wonder Tony Soprano was always lamenting the demise of the strong, silent Gary Cooper type. Where have they all gone? Many of the posts I came across were written by men scared of their own shadow. I wouldn't trust them to handle a toothbrush, let alone a newborn baby. Like traumatised rabbits caught in the glare of oncoming headlights, they pose question after question and more dos and don'ts than a nuclear bomb dismantling kit. If they were not installing Big Brother-like "nanny cams" above the baby's cot, they were asking questions like "I'm having a baby with my partner but her jealous ex-husband is a really big bloke, what should I do?" and "My wife can't breastfeed and obviously I can't either. Can anyone help?"

Within minutes, I felt like a shameful, seedy voyeur for reading the trials and tribulations of expectant and new fathers I didn't know and a useless wet rag for going to that website in the first place. This feeling intensified after reading one guy's essay on breastfeeding, which might as well have been titled "The life and times of my wife's enormous knockers", as he rambled on about nipple length, colour and overall soreness. I haven't met this bloke or anyone in his family but, by the time I had finished, I felt like I knew his wife's breasts intimately.

Another father insisted that we all take a moment to reflect on how fortunate we were to be blessed by the power of procreation by pondering the predicament of those who had fallen by the wayside. He opted for subtlety by posting up every patronising lyric of "Another Day in Paradise" by Phil Collins. Oh, think twice. Think twice, daddies.

I closed the website. No longer feeling guilty, I was slightly alarmed. Just when had men turned into a studio audience on *Dr. Phil*? We used to be good at making babies. We did it naturally, often in caves and in total darkness. Darwin wrote a book all about it. Now we need nanny cams connected up to our flat-screen TVs.

Of course, all this ranting is my unconvincing smokescreen. A product of my generation, raised by a nanny state and the constant intervention of third parties, my initial reaction to the nanny cam was "Oh, that would be pretty good to have above little Eraser's head" when I know that my father's—and particularly my grandfather's— reaction would be, "A nanny cam? What the hell do you need one of those for?"

My father wouldn't have been trawling through websites for expectant fathers to lessen any sense of guilt for being away temporarily from his pregnant wife. He was too busy working on a building site every morning from 7 a.m. That was his job, along with dancing around the delivery room shouting, "It's a boy, it's a boy" and throwing his six-month-old son towards the ceiling at breathtaking speed after his beloved West Ham United lifted the FA Cup. This is not criticism. That's what fathers were for in 1974.

No, I must toughen up. I'm a boy from Dagenham. I've been mugged twice at knifepoint and I've been punched on the jaw by a drunk, middle-aged football hooligan. (He was a fellow West Ham supporter who had hobbled over on crutches but that is not the point.) From now on, I need to be a bit less Dr. Phil and a bit more like that guy in that famous Rudyard Kipling poem.

Saturday, 27 October

The poem I was struggling to remember is called *If.* I tracked down the epic ode to stiff upper lip, Victorian stoicism on the Internet this morning. I read it through twice and cried my eyes out, accompanied by an extremely wobbly lower lip. My child will run rings around me.

Tuesday, 30 October

Over the past two weeks, old friends and colleagues in Singapore have been asking the one question I know the answer to but cannot let on. When is Humphreys Junior coming? One or two jokingly suggested that I still needed a learner's permit in the bedroom. Every nerve and sinew within me fought the urge to turn into Bo Diddley and shout, "I'm a Man! And I've got three positive pregnancy tests to prove it!"

Instead, I merely smiled politely and churned out one rehearsed cliché after another: We're still finding our feet in a new country; Don't worry, you'll be the first to know; My wife's re-establishing her career in Australia; I'm a Jaffa orange.

Telling people, particularly those I barely know, that I am seedless is the quickest conversation stopper. It's not politically (or anatomically) correct but it saves a lot of time, garners sympathy and, if I'm lucky, a concerned female hand on the arm.

Today, I told a stranger at a festival event that the seedless streak was genetic.

"Yeah, I can't seem to hit the target," I said, with all the mock earnestness I could muster. "Unfortunately, this seedless streak runs in the family. My father was the same."

"Oh, really," came the sympathetic reply followed by the concerned hand on the arm. "That's terrible."

Yes, it was terrible and I will probably burn in hell for all eternity, but hey, I'm having a baby but can't tell anyone so I'll take my kicks where I can get 'em. Besides, I know the truth.

I'm Bo Diddley. I'm a Man.

Thursday, 1 November

There was an emotional reunion at Melbourne Airport's Terminal 2 with my wife and the pencil-top eraser at 6.30 a.m. The poor woman looked exhausted. She smiled, rubbed her stomach and asked if I had noticed the lump. I lied and said yes. She was tired, nauseous and had got up at 5 a.m. to pick up her husband, who had done little more than attend several concerts and literature workshops in the past fortnight. In contrast, she had spent much of that time lying on our sofa with a bucket for company.

I did not have the heart to tell the truth. She had actually lost weight and her shrunken, gaunt physical appearance had taken me aback. Getting by on nothing other than toast, cups of tea (something she never usually drank) and the odd yoghurt for two weeks had taken its toll. We soon discovered that for some women the first two months of pregnancy can be a great weight loss programme. My wife was no exception. I, on the other hand, had compensated for her finicky appetite by eating my way around Singapore.

Just a few hours and a quick nap later, we were back in the two-finger typist's office. It was almost two months and time for a routine check-up. This was the chance I had been waiting for—a chance for my ignorance of the pregnancy process to really shine.

"So what do we do now, doctor?" I asked the moment I sat down so he didn't have a chance to bang out another half a dozen emails or Google his next holiday package.

"Well, we'll do a physical check, make sure everything feels OK around the womb and then we'll think about an obstetrician."

I looked at my wife. She was nodding along in agreement with the doctor.

"How do we go about finding a local obstetrician?" my wife replied. "Do we find one or do you refer us to one?"

"As you're new to the area, we can recommend a few who have proved popular in the past and you can choose one."

During this scene, my head turned left and right like a confused kid watching his first tennis match as the two protagonists carried out their conversation. I was desperate to halt proceedings by shouting, "Will someone please tell me what the fuck an obstetrician is?"

I know now. Thanks to the combination of my eternally patient wife and Wikipedia, I am now fully aware that an obstetrician specialises in pregnancy and the eventual delivery. I can even type the word without the assistance of spell checker. At the time, however, I was appalled by my obtuseness. It's not as if I lacked all understanding of that side of the medical profession. Thanks to British stand-up comics and a hackneyed old joke, I'd known what a gynaecologist did since childhood ("I'm not a gynaecologist, darling, but I'll have a bloody good look at it for you"). But obstetrics? That was the field of NASA astronauts, surely.

"You can get the names of the obstetricians from the receptionist when we're done. OK then, why not pop onto the bed and take your clothes off," said the suddenly chirpy doctor. "I'll nip outside for a couple of minutes to give you time to get undressed."

I appreciated the doctor's efforts to protect my wife's dignity but he seemed to disappear more often than the Scarlet Pimpernel. My wife, who has never felt the least bit embarrassed when it comes to these kinds of examinations, whipped off her clothes so fast I thought they were attached by Velcro. She stretched out on the bed, naked from the waist down and said, "It's exciting, isn't it?"

"You're lying there with your bits out waiting for a middle-aged man to return with a pair of surgical gloves and some jelly. How excited would you like me to be?"

"You know what I mean."

I did, but I still admired her relaxed demeanour. Shortly before leaving Singapore, I came down with a rash around my testicles. There's no punchline coming. I really did come down with a rash around my testicles. Driven to the brink of castration by the persistent itching, I made an appointment to see a doctor with the utmost reluctance. In an attempt to allay my fears and potential humiliation, I reminded myself that the doctor was a buffed, rugby-playing Chinese chap—a man's man, one of the lads. We'd discuss my problem, gloss over it quickly and discuss the weekend's English Premier League fixtures. It would be as if the image of a man cupping my balls in his hand had never been a reality.

Imagine my horror, then, when I stepped into the doctor's office only to find that he was a she, and a rather attractive Chinese lady in her late thirties at that. This is the stuff that nightmares and Jerry Springer episodes are made of. The last time my sensitive area had been examined in any detail by a woman was by my mother sometime after my tenth birthday. I had been suffering from intense groin pains caused by a late tackle in a Sunday morning football match (that's my story and I'm sticking to it). My mum had a cursory look, told me to toughen up and returned to the living room to inform all her friends at the Tupperware party that "my son is growing hairs".

In the end, the doctor behaved in the appropriate fashion, examining my testicles with utter indifference while discussing the need to apply cream when venturing into Singapore's rainforest. I feigned interest by nodding in all the right places but what I was actually thinking was "Don't you move a bloody muscle."

My mature, half-naked wife had no such qualms. Lying back and thinking of England, she wondered again if we should inform our parents.

"I thought we had agreed on Christmas Day," I said.

"You did. I still think it's too late," she replied while probing for lumps and depressions.

"Well, what about my birthday then as a compromise?" It's in early December, a few weeks before Christmas but slightly after the three-month period.

"I'll think about it."

At that moment, I noticed an elderly woman outside in the street waddle past the window. I jumped up.

"Did you see that?"

"See what?"

"That old woman wandering past the window through the gap in the blinds."

"No, I was looking at my belly. Do you think it looks slightly bigger on one side?"

"If I can see out, then people can see in. I don't want the entire street staring at your bits through the window. Quick, cover yourself up."

Not the least bit concerned, my wife pulled a sheet over her legs and continued to prod gently at her stomach. After presumably nipping into the chemist, the doctor finally returned with a tube of jelly. I got up to leave.

"Do you want me to wait outside, doctor?"

"Not at all, not at all," the gloved one replied, ushering me back to my seat. I'd never seen him so happy. "Of course you should stay. We all want to see how baby's doing."

Indeed we did. But we didn't all want to see where that jelly was going.

"That all feels nice and healthy," I heard the doctor say as I took a profound interest in an elderly chap removing his bicycle clips out in the street. "The pelvis could be a bit narrow though."

Putting aside my immature Victorian conservatism for a moment, I glanced over. The doctor was pressing softly around my wife's pelvis.

"Will that be a problem, doctor?" my wife asked, immediately betraying her concern.

"Probably not. But you might want to consult your obstetrician about it."

Why? I thought. How's a bloody astronaut going to help?

Friday, 2 November

Eight weeks today and it's the size of a strawberry. Today, our little strawberry officially becomes a foetus. All the major systems and organ systems should have formed and my wife is now carrying a little person with an outrageously large head. More importantly, the likelihood of miscarrying decreases every week from now on. We have produced a foetus that now has its own face. Little strawberry has a face; a tiny cherubic face on the front of a shockingly enormous head that resembles the Mekon in *Dan Dare* comics.

Sunday, 4 November

Today has been the worst day so far. It was just wretched. Little strawberry really did behave like the fiendish Mekon. My wife left the bed only to urinate (on the hour, every hour) and retch (on the half hour). At all other times, she clutched her stomach, winced in pain or slept fitfully. Frustration in the morning gave way to tears in the afternoon and finally resignation. My wife cried not because of the considerable discomfort, but because of the guilt at being so dependent. Getting a glass of water was an insurmountable task, the few steps from the bedroom to the kitchen clearly beyond her. She tried. She never stopped trying.

Yet her failed attempts to complete any of the most basic of chores only exacerbated the wretched feeling of dependency. She tried to get dressed but ended up back in bed and cried. She gamely attempted walking into the living room, started heaving violently and ended up back in bed. She capitalised on her sudden craving for toast, took one bite and ended up face down in the toilet bowl. She could sleep. She could pee. That was it. Even a newborn baby can eat.

When she was awake and not gagging, she was apologising. Sorry for not getting out of bed. Sorry for not helping with the shopping, the cooking, the cleaning, the mopping and the sweeping. Although we probably shouldn't get carried away with the cooking. My cuisine consists of various tinned foods on toast and instant noodles. I'm hardly a threat to Jamie Oliver.

Pregnancy books always point out that between about six and sixteen weeks, the pregnant woman may feel nauseous. Just like that. You may feel nauseous, ladies. It's almost an off-hand afterthought, suggesting the odd tummy ache and an extended stay on the toilet. You may feel nauseous, ladies. That's all. You may feel like someone is smacking you in the stomach with a cricket bat, pouring liquid soap into your mouth and smothering all your meals with stray cat faeces, ladies. That's all.

Most pregnancy books, or most of the pregnancy books that I flicked through at least, mentioned the nausea but rarely emphasised the sense of worthlessness. My wife felt worthless today. Fiercely independent, she couldn't fend for herself and that frustration led to the tears. It wasn't the nausea itself, but the inability to execute her decisions. She settled on toast but couldn't make it. She wanted some fresh air but couldn't reach the door. She felt unclean and decided to shower but couldn't get to the bathroom without gagging. She was a slave to the actions of others (in this case, me) and it was an impossible situation for both of us. She felt worthless. I felt useless.

My wife has spent a large portion of the day crying herself to sleep and I have not been able to do anything other than offer hollow words of comfort. "It'll get better," I said. "It'll pass," I said. "You'll bounce back after a good's night sleep," I said. What did I know? I hadn't even known what an obstetrician was until recently. How could I expect her to be reassured when I didn't believe what I was saying? In almost fifteen years, I had never seen my formidable partner so weak and fragile. Even a gentle embrace made her wince. My soulmate was in constant pain and I had nothing to offer except empty promises.

When a loved one is sick, people often say that just being there is enough.

It isn't.

Friday, 9 November

Nine weeks today. We should have a medium green olive now that is stretching out towards 30 mm.

The gagging and retching come and go but the nausea and the exhaustion are omnipresent. My wife's determination to get out of bed every morning to teach 25 preschoolers has been nothing short of heroic. Most evenings, she returns home, eats some toast and slumps straight into bed. She usually nods off before sunset and sleeps in way past sunrise. But she's getting there. Through gritted teeth and the occasional cry of "For fuck's sake, Neil, let me rest", she is getting there.

So let's talk about belly rubbing. I noticed, almost in passing, that my wife had taken to rubbing her stomach almost within hours of those two lines appearing in the first pregnancy test. Now she rubs more often than Aladdin. She's not aware that she's doing it half the time. It's a subconscious maternal instinct, almost primal, and I find it wonderfully endearing. She finds it comforting.

The rubbing does veer towards the obsessive at times, though, and bordered on the competitive this morning. We were in the supermarket examining those cute little jars of baby food—again—when another pregnant couple headed down the aisle. The mother-to-be clearly didn't have much further to go. She had that *March of the Penguins* waddle down to a T and was wearing those baggy dungarees that all pregnant women must wear, by law, in the third trimester. Examining all-in-one shampoo and conditioner with one hand, she was instinctively rubbing her bump in a circular motion with the other.

"Here, look at that woman. The one dressed like a children's entertainer," I whispered. "She's rubbing her belly."

"Yeah ... well? I rub my belly, too," replied my distinctly unimpressed wife.

"I know you do. She just seems to be ..."

"Seems to be what?"

"Well, you know, because she's almost due, she's rubbing her belly a bit more."

"I rub my belly all the time. You just don't see me. When I'm at work, I rub it all the time. I'm always rubbing Little Olive."

But I was fascinated by the constant tummy rubbing and later did a search on the Internet. The results were intriguing. After typing in "belly-rubbing pregnancy", I discovered that Holly Madison might be pregnant! The exclamation mark comes courtesy of the celebrity gossip website. I didn't even know who Holly Madison was. Reading on, I discovered that Madison was a Playboy Playmate and one of Hugh Hefner's three girlfriends. The man's over 80, for heaven's sake. If I'm still here at 80, I strongly suspect there will be more chance of raising the *Titanic*. Old Hef, on the other hand, cannot only get it up for three different women but is still capable of producing little "Heffers" apparently. According to the website, Madison was spotted wearing loose clothes and rubbing her belly outside a swanky lounge in Los Angeles. I always said my wife had a lot in common with those Playboy bunnies.

A click later and I was in Italy, where they believe that rubbing a pregnant woman's tummy brings good luck. I later rubbed my wife's bump repeatedly. I felt it was the right thing to do. West Ham faces a potential banana skin away to Derby County tomorrow.

Finally, I came across an entertaining step-by-step guide entitled "How to Keep Strangers from Touching Your Tummy When Pregnant". There were various options, scenarios and choices depending on the situation. My wife could smile demurely and feign shyness, pretend she's ticklish or that she suffers from some kind of contagious, repulsive skin rash. If the latter was true, one suspects she'd only be fighting off strangers in white coats and surgical masks. My favourite tip was to reach out for the stranger's stomach as they reach out for yours, like a kind of mutual exchange. Should a neighbour pat our foetus gently, I really cannot see my wife slapping his beer belly and saying, "Woah, how long has it been now? Twenty years? Yeah, you can really see the beer belly swelling now. You must both be so proud. When's the liver failure due?"

Sunday, 11 November

West Ham stuffed Derby County 5–0 last night. It was one of their biggest away victories in recent memory. I spent the day chasing my nauseous wife around the house in a desperate attempt to rub her bump. I had my reasons. The Hammers are away to the old enemy Tottenham Hotspur in a couple of weeks. My wife told me where to go. She had her reasons.

Tuesday, 13 November

Today was a historic day in the household, a truly proud moment for the mum-to-be. After another weekend of appalling nausea and overwhelming tiredness, she perked up considerably. In fact, in one startling moment of physical exertion, she even performed a little dance outside the bathroom. She needed a lengthy lie-down immediately after, but I hadn't witnessed such an energetic outburst in weeks. But then, she had good reason to be cheerful. She had made a decisive breakthrough in the pregnancy. She had finally vomited.

And I mean proper vomiting. None of that gagging followed by a teaspoonful of saliva—this was the real deal. The shaking shoulders, the shrinking head, the eyes on stalks and the Swahili yodel. This was throwing up at its finest and my wife could not be happier.

When her finest hour arrived, I was in the living room watching the English Premier League highlights show.

"Neil, come here quickly," her moaning, dislocated voice echoed around the house.

"Yeah, all right, I'm coming," I replied, and returned to my inertia. I told you how many West Ham won by, right?

"Neil, come here, now! And bring a plastic bag with you."

"What have you broken this time?"

"Just bring the bag here now."

That made me move. I grabbed a bag and ran to the toilet,

where my wife had buried her head halfway up the U-bend.

"What's the matter, mate?" I asked.

"I've been sick," she mumbled weakly. "Real sick this time. I came into the bathroom and ... BLUEGH!"

And she was sick again. This was Niagara Falls meets Linda Blair. It was incessant. Where was it all coming from? I was convinced someone had taken a hosepipe from a nearby drain and shoved it up my wife's backside. I had never seen so much fluid come out from such a small person. I harboured fears that my wife was dissipating before my very eyes and all I'd be left with was a pile of clothes and a wet patch.

The plastic bag, I assumed, was to catch the vomit, but there just wasn't the time. Feeling even more irrelevant than usual, I dropped the bag and rubbed my wife's back. My jelly-like wife eventually collapsed in a heap on the bathroom floor and I cleaned up the mess around the bowl. I do not wish to sound vulgar here but where do all those carrots come from? It was like being married to Bugs Bunny.

Then we had a Kafka moment. There was a metamorphosis. My zombie-like wife turned into an aerobics instructor. She jumped up, kissed me on the cheek (which almost had me diving into the toilet bowl as she had the distinct whiff of stale vomit about her) and danced into the hallway singing, "I finally vomited! I finally vomited!"

"Well, you've suddenly come alive," I remarked, genuinely taken aback. "Why are you so cheerful?"

"I've finally vomited," she cried, as she danced into another room. "I'm proper pregnant now."

"You were proper pregnant before," I shouted, as I held my nose and sprayed a Toilet Duck bottle like a graffiti artist all around the room.

"No, but I was only doing all that spitting. Now it's proper vomiting. So I'm happy. I'm right on track. I've got proper morning sickness now."

"That's great, mate. I'm really pleased for you," I shouted back. "Do you think you can hold back on the carrots from now on then?"

Friday, 16 November

Ten weeks. If all is going well, the baby weighs about 5 g and is the size of a small plum. I childishly spent the day telling my wife that she had a little plum hanging down between her legs.

Friday, 23 November

Eleven weeks. We have a large lime with a grossly outsized head. It *is* the lime-green Mekon now. My wife is looking forward to a growth spurt as the length of the foetus is likely to double in the next three weeks. Bring on the stretch marks.

Saturday, 24 November

I learnt an important lesson about impending fatherhood today so here's a quick note to prospective dads. Whenever your partner rubs her bump, resist the temptation to shout, "Bring on the stretch marks."

Monday, 26 November

West Ham managed a scrappy draw away to Tottenham Hotspur last night. Bloody Italians and their daft old wives' tales about rubbing bellies.

Tuesday, 27 November

We have an official bump. There is no mistaking it now. For a few weeks now, my wife has been jutting out her stomach to accentuate a bump that was not really there, making her look more like the letter *D* than a pregnant woman. She has *felt* the bump for at least a month and has therefore convinced herself that she can actually *see* it. I rather obstinately insisted that the bump might have been her imagination, not because I get a kick out of playing an inconsiderate sourpuss but because there really wasn't a bump there. I'd seen bigger bumps on my wife's "water retention" days. Now I've never been quite sure of the science or the trigger factors behind a female's water retention but the symptoms invariably appear after a Pizza Hut buffet.

Today wasn't a water retention bump day. Today was our large lime subtly announcing its presence to the world. It's not significant. It's still easily hidden beneath clothes, but it's a sign that a little Humphreys is on its way. My wife undressed this evening to get into the shower and I suddenly went all silly and giggly. In fairness, I have gone all silly and giggly at such a routine occurrence for years. But this was different. I noticed the presence of my unborn child for the first time. It was a timeless moment. So, characteristically, I went rather hysterical.

"What are you laughing at," my confused wife asked as she slipped into pyjamas with an elastic waistband that will prove increasingly useful.

"I can see your bump. Hee hee," I replied, giggling and practically covering my mouth. I was back in kindergarten again, tittering away in the changing room and making comments like "I can see your sausage. Hee hee." That's a tip I'm certainly going to pass on to my large lime if it's a boy. When you stand in a school dressing room, son, never make a comment on anything witnessed in that room. Whether it relates to length, girth or texture, keep it to yourself, son. Oh, one more thing. Never, ever stand next to the kid whose sausage suggests he was sired by Seabiscuit.

"Of course, there's a bump. I've been telling you that for weeks," she said. Attempts to sound exasperated failed miserably. She was obviously delighted that the bump was no longer the property of her fertile imagination. She smiled, rubbed her bump and invited me over to do likewise.

Now I can't stop smiling either.

Wednesday, 28 November

Baby documentaries. They are never off the TV now. In truth, they were rarely off the TV before but the audience dynamics have changed. I have to watch them now. I walked into the living room this afternoon and was confronted by the sight of a panting woman in her forties (who perhaps should have known better) giving birth to triplets. According to my commentary-providing wife, the woman's triplets were the result of IVF treatment, and a touch of insanity no doubt.

Our TV is a reasonably wide flat screen, my only technological indulgence. From the moment I knew such widescreen contraptions were available, I wanted one to watch Luke Skywalker's X-wing dive into the Death Star trench. I had not spent my savings to watch a cervix push out three bloody babies past a pair of chubby thighs. I don't know if you've ever watched a pair of chubby thighs on a 42-inch LCD screen, but I can see why they only show Pixar cartoons and rock concerts at most TV showrooms.

My wife beckoned me over to join her on the sofa, pointing out that the documentary ain't over till the fat lady pushes out her third baby. Normally, I would make my apologies and attend to a more pressing engagement, like cleaning out my toenails with a fork.

"But you've got to watch it," my wife insisted, producing her trump card. "Our baby wants you to watch it."

From this day on, I shall always be in the minority. I will be involved in all house discussions, debates and votes but the balance of power will never be tipped in my favour. I now know how Britain's Liberal Democrats feel. I hold a vote. My wife holds a vote. Our unborn child now holds a vote apparently. My wife controls the unborn child and, ipso facto, controls the house. She holds a literal and moral majority now. What kind of man goes against the wishes of an embryo?

"What do you mean the baby wants me to watch it?" I ventured. "Don't talk rubbish."

"Come on, mate. Come and sit with us."

The house majority had spoken. So I sat and stared at a woman's cervix being stretched wide enough apart to deliver three babies. I should have got drunk on the intoxicating experience, the creation of life, the beauty of birth. I could have pacified my wife by churning out a couple of clichés like "the end result is worth the pain and the sacrifice" or "the protracted labour will mean nothing once the baby is delivered to your arms". I should have said any one of those things. But I didn't. Instead, I spent several, terrifying minutes staring at the woman's dilated cervix. Deep, dark and cavernous, it reminded me of a London Underground tunnel. I half expected to be dazzled by lights before the District Line service to Upminster trundled through. So rather than reassure my pregnant wife about the traumatic ordeal of delivering a baby, I fixated on this poor woman's cervix and found myself asking, "When this is all over, I'm going to feel like a conductor's baton waving about in the Royal Albert Hall, aren't I?"

We watched the rest of the documentary in silence.

Friday, 30 November

Twelve weeks today. It is as long as a matchbox now.

The nausea persists with devilish stubbornness but with growing infrequency, which is most welcome. When the symptoms are particularly acute, my wife's well-rehearsed routine is to lie on the sofa and watch those pre-recorded documentaries depicting women giving birth. She finds it therapeutic. I find it disturbing. These documentary guinea pigs are the kind of women who have no problems with a camera crew using a harsh lens to zoom in on their vaginas. My wife insists their presence in the living room is reassuring. I'm pleased, but I can't help wondering how the sight of screaming, breathless women is comforting. Why doesn't she stick with Jerry Springer?

Sunday, 1 December

My wife is growing eyelids for our matchbox. She sat on the sofa for much of the afternoon and, between pregnancy programmes on Discovery's Home and Health Channel, made a pair of eyelids. This is her latest line. If there is a household chore that involves an extra pair of hands, a door to be opened or a phone to be answered, she's too busy producing a new body part.

"Can you get that, mate," I called out this morning from the top of a ladder as the phone rang. "I'm up the top of a ladder."

"I can't. I'm busy making our matchbox a pair of eyelids at the moment."

"Can you hold back a minute and get the phone? I'm up a ladder trying to hang up the three Christmas stockings you insisted on."

"We've got to have one for the matchbox, haven't we?"

"Why? It hasn't got any eyelids yet, apparently, but it needs a stocking."

"Our baby will have eyelids if you stop pestering me."

Bloody pregnancy books. My wife bought a mother-to-be's beautifully presented, handmade day-to-day journal from one of those shops filled with joss sticks, incense, potpourri and therapeutic candles that offer a hundred different aromas but all contain a definite aroma of urine. This particular "companion" (these things are always called a "companion", a "partner", a "keepsake" or a "mother's memento" as no one ever thinks to call a pregnancy book "a book" anymore) includes the stages of foetal growth. At this stage, the foetus is growing eyelids. At this stage, the foetus's teeth are budding in the gums. At this stage, the foetus is developing an interest in the forthcoming primaries for the American presidency. That sort of thing.

My wife has unilaterally established a unique division of labour in the house. I put up the Christmas decorations, including an extra stocking for our unborn matchbox, the tree and the tinsel, vacuum the carpet to remove all traces of superfluous tinsel and plastic leaves and make a spectacularly mediocre dinner that involves only a microwave and a tin opener while my wife helps our unborn child develop eyelids. Sounds fair to me.

Tuesday, 4 December

D-Day. Doctor day. Our first trip to see the baby doctor. The obstetrician. Until very recently, I had no idea what an obstetrician's field of medical expertise encompassed. After several fruitless phone calls, I concluded that his duties included employing obstreperous receptionists. I also concluded that there are not enough obstetricians in the world. When I was a teenager and plotting my career path, my every waking moment was preoccupied with female genitalia and spending as much time around it as possible. Thankfully, my friends and I were blissfully unaware of the job requirements of the average obstetrician or we might now be delivering more babies than China. But it certainly wouldn't hurt if a few more careers guidance counsellors threw up the option of obstetrics, judging by the profession's desperate shortage of practitioners in my town.

I called the first three in the *Yellow Pages* and was politely informed by each of the surgeries that they couldn't see us for our first all-important twelve-week scan for at least another three weeks which, I ventured, would have undermined the purpose and relevance of the twelve-week scan. My fourth call, to a surgery recommended by our local GP, was a wonderfully short and brusque exchange.

"Hello, my wife is pregnant and heading towards twelve weeks. We were wondering if we could make an appointment with your obstetrician?" I asked, with as much politeness as I could muster after three rejections.

"No."

"I'm sorry?"

"No, you can't."

"We can't what?"

"You can't see our obstetrician."

"Why is that?"

"Because she's not an obstetrician anymore. She stopped practising about three years ago." The woman's disgusted tone suggested that the doctor had once been involved in the dark arts.

"So, she's not an obstetrician anymore then?"

"No."

"And there's no other obstetrician at your surgery?"

"No."

"And when she gave up on obstetrics, you gave up on your social skills?"

The woman at the fifth surgery said she could add us to their patients' roster but that the next available appointment—and I swear on my unborn matchbox that she actually said this—was in May. Five months from now. If my wife waddled in to the doctor's surgery and declared she was ready for her twelve-week scan then, he'd be straight on the phone to all the women's magazines. I was almost ready to give up.

Finally, thanks to a cancellation, a certain Dr Derek managed to squeeze us in.

Dr Derek was born to be an obstetrician and not for the teenage, puerile sexual reasons either. I'm sure he's like the stand-up comedian who comes home after work and says, "If one more stranger tells me a bloody joke ..." No, Dr Derek was born to be an obstetrician because of his incomparable bedside manner. His office was filled with photographs of delighted parents: shots of flushed, exhausted mothers proudly clutching their offspring while the fathers stared goofily at their newborn and, of course, Dr Derek sandwiched between the parents. The guy has appeared in photographs with children more times than Ronald McDonald. And the parents clearly could not get enough of him. The walls were adorned with gushing thank you notes and letters informing Dr Derek of the baby's latest developments and achievements. One or two of the notes were even written by the children themselves (several years had obviously elapsed; Dr Derek has not delivered freaks or anything). It was extraordinary. No doctor could be this popular, surely. And then Dr Derek spoke, and I momentarily pondered the merits of homosexuality and considered asking him to do likewise.

In soft, dulcet tones that belonged on a late-night, Dr Love-type radio show, he said, "You're finally here. You're on the road to having a baby. There will be lots of questions and I will try to provide all the answers. But we will get through it together. I will be with you all the way. I will deliver your baby. His name will be Kal-El. He will eradicate global poverty, end the reigns of African despots and bring lasting peace to the Middle East. He will stand together with Bono and Geldof and release the greatest charity CD single in history. And I will be at his side as it happens."

I might not have quoted Dr Derek's opening monologue verbatim but I drifted away when he promised to provide all the answers, his comforting words of reassurance lifting me to a higher spiritual plane with visions of my offspring singing with U2 at Wembley. The good doctor was good. He was very, very good. If he ran for presidency, for absolutely anything, I'd cross his box without a moment's hesitation.

Dr Derek touched my wife's arm. He did this a lot. I was a trifle concerned by my initial reaction. He hasn't touched my arm once, I thought.

"OK, then. Would you like to see your baby?" he asked rhetorically, in that butter-soft voice of his. "Just lie back on the bed there and lift your shirt up a bit."

My wife has never undressed so quickly for another man before. Dr Derek squeezed some gel over the little bump and went to work with his little hand-held transducer across my wife's uterus. Our first ultrasound scan had begun.

"Just stare over at the monitor there," said Dr Derek, in the sultriest of voices usually reserved for disc jockey spiel like "and here's Chris De Burgh's 'Lady in Red' for Ross in Cotton Street who's home alone with the latest issue of *Playboy*".

We stared intently at the monitor. For a few moments, it was fuzzy as Dr Derek zigzagged below my wife's belly button. And there it was. It was hazy at first, like a TV picture with weak reception, but then the snow disappeared and, for a fleeting moment, the image was clear. It wasn't a matchbox or a lime. It wasn't even an embryo or a foetus. It was a baby. It was our baby. Right there in front of us, performing the kind of acrobatics usually seen by prepubescent girls from Eastern Europe at the Olympics. It was our baby, our baby the Olympic gymnast. From now on, it could only be our baby. My wife and I looked at each other and laughed hysterically. There were no tears, just lots of laughter. Each time our baby flipped, and it flipped around more times than a dolphin, we giggled all over again. Our reaction was natural and instinctive and the right one. Tears and heartfelt hugs are for Hallmark movies and Mills and Boon novels. Our healthy-looking baby was jumping around like a firecracker on the fourth of July and it was the funniest sight.

"That's its leg there," said the soothing one, shifting position with his gizmo. "And there's the other one now, coming across the top of it."

That was the most surreal, and certainly the most emotional, moment. Seemingly playing for the camera, this three-month-old being did something that I have been doing for over thirty years and my own father for over fifty. Our baby fidgeted with its feet.

My father has always rubbed his feet together, particularly when he's distracted or excited, so needless to say there has been some serious sock friction over the years. If he's watching West Ham and they suddenly score against the run of the play, he can practically make fire. I have inherited my father's physical tic. Equally long-legged and equally fidgety, I lie back on the sofa while my feet audition for *Riverdance*.

"You're doing it again," my irritated wife likes to point out during commercial breaks. "Keep your feet still."

"Sorry. I don't even know I'm doing it. Especially if I'm watching the TV."

A pause.

"Keep your bloody legs still."

Dr Derek froze the baby's image on the monitor to take a couple of measurements. Its length was 7.78 cm. Dr Derek suggested the baby might be further along than 12½ weeks. Then he studied my 1.94-m frame and corrected himself. He returned to his computer and flicked a switch. The room was suddenly engulfed by a rhythmic, other-worldly drone. The aliens had landed. It was *War of the Worlds* in the doctor's office. They were drawing up their plans against us.

"That's the baby's heartbeat echoing around the room," said Dr Derek, sensing our uncertainty.

"Thank God for that. I thought the mother ship had returned," I muttered.

"It's producing 149 heartbeats a minute."

"Yeah, so am I," I replied.

He allowed our baby's heartbeat to reverberate around the room for a few more seconds. We giggled again. The measured sound really was wonderful. But I did expect Elliot to burst through the door on his BMX with E.T. in a wicker basket.

Dr Derek assured us, again, that everything was on track and that nothing had popped up on the scan to warrant any concern.

Nevertheless, I asked for the optional nuchal translucency test for personal reasons. The nuchal translucency test measures the thickness of the soft tissue on the back of a baby's neck. Around this period, various abnormalities, including Down's syndrome, can cause a larger nuchal translucency, which can be picked up by an ultrasound scan. After Dr Derek's receptionist arranged an appointment with a sonographer who specialised in nuchal translucency scans, the doctor patted my wife's arm a few more times and sent us on our way with a priceless souvenir: four scan images of our acrobatic baby demonstrating its powers of contortion.

The photographs are currently sitting on my desk. I can't stop looking at them.

Wednesday, 5 December

I'm 33 today. If all goes to plan, by the time I'm 34, I will be the father of an incorrigible foot-fidget.

My mother called in the evening from England to tell me, once again, that she went into labour on Thursday, 5 December 1974 during an episode of *Top of the Pops*. She castigated me, once again, for making her rush to the hospital before she could find out what that week's No.1 single was. Leaving before the country's most popular music programme had finished, she locked the door to her small flat above a bike shop in North London and headed to the hospital on a bus. A bloody bus! The fortitude of my mother's generation continues to embarrass me. My wife and I recently spent several hours wondering whether or not to buy a new car for no other reason than our current, fuel-efficient, low carbon-emissions vehicle will struggle to fit a baby's pram in its boot. Exactly 33 years earlier, my swollen mother flagged down a London bus because she couldn't be bothered to wait for a taxi. She had been experiencing twinges for most of the afternoon but decided to make my dad and her brother dinner first before pushing me out.

There were no monthly ultrasound scans, no regular visits with a suave, arm-patting obstetrician and no two-car families. My dad rushed home from a building site on the Tube and took my twenty-year-old mum to hospital on a London bus. That's how I came into the world: uncomplicated, no frills and no different to every other child born into a working-class family in the 1970s. Today, we get our pregnancy and parenthood tips from glossy magazines and daytime TV. It's hard not to feel like a bit of a wanker really.

Thursday, 6 December

But I did make a baby and the desire to tell the world is overwhelming. I am Man, I make fire (when I rub my feet together), I make baby and my birthday had been the date earmarked to go public.

We chickened out. It was largely my doing. I am a fastidious worrier at the best of times and abhor loose ends, and the nuchal translucency test is a significant loose end. Yet at the same time, I had the irrepressible urge to announce to the world that my sperm had taken off like Michael Phelps and hit the target with astounding speed and efficiency.

Now, I'll readily put my hand up and admit that this is a childish, trivial and largely irrelevant reason to tell your relatives that another addition to the family is on its way. My wife's health and that of the baby—ten fingers and toes and all that—supersede all other concerns. I know that. But the temptation to inform all and sundry that conception was faster than a shot from a canon is difficult to resist.

The maths is simple enough. In July, we agreed that even though Australia was our third country of residence in just over ten years, we were as settled as two itchy wanderers could be and decided to stop using contraception.

In August, my mother, stepfather and youngest brother arrived and stayed for a month. Call me old-fashioned, but my baby-making responsibilities were put on hold the moment my mother temporarily moved into the bedroom next door. If I could hear her snoring in her bedroom, then … I'm not even going to go there.

In September, we resumed our efforts to create a "plus one" in the household. On 5 October, two lines popped up in the square window. That's all I'm going to say. Along with two words: medical marvel.

The Second Trimester

Friday, 7 December

Thirteen weeks today. We've had the sex, now we're on the honeymoon. It's all different nowadays. We have reached the end of the first trimester. With a relatively complication-free pregnancy so far, our risk of miscarriage should be around 2 per cent as we move into the second trimester. The second trimester is often referred to as the honeymoon phase of pregnancy. Women bloom, bumps show and faces glow. According to the pregnancy books, the nausea and omnipresent fatigue should be subsiding by now. My wife celebrated the news by spending most of the evening on the sofa feeling sick and swearing at me. So much for the books.

Monday, 10 December

"I must, I must improve my bust." "I must, I must improve my bust." That is the new household mantra. My wife is beginning to feel tight, stretching pains under her belly button. She feels like she is being used in a tug of war contest and her uterus is the rope, with half a dozen burly men pulling at it in opposite directions. Her uterus is expanding rapidly. Soon it will be bigger than a fist. She is convinced her uterus is bigger than a beach ball. I asked her what the pulling and stretching feel like.

"You know those daft chest expanders that women use in gyms, thinking they will make their boobs bigger?" she asked. "Those springy things?"

"Yeah, my mum always said, 'I must, I must improve my bust'".

"Yeah, so did my mum. Weird. Well, it feels like that. My belly is a chest expander."

"I must, I must improve my bust."

"Exactly."

If she's in another room and I hear a stifled groan, I call out and ask, "I must, I must improve my bust?"

"Yeah."

"Thought so."

God knows what the neighbours think.

Tuesday, 11 December

On a whim, I did a Google search for "I must, I must improve my bust." The slogan pops up everywhere: in headlines, on beauty websites and in countless articles on breast enlargements. Where did it come from? I must ask my mother.

Wednesday, 12 December

She didn't know either. But it didn't stop her repeating the phrase to me down the phone. Has your mother ever said "I must, I must improve my bust" to you at regular intervals? It is not good.

Thursday, 13 December

The mantra comes from Judy Blume's coming-of-age book *Are You There God? It's Me, Margaret*, which follows the teenager's quest to reconcile her mixed religious heritage. Apparently, young Margaret performs chest exercises with her mates in a desperate bid for bigger boobs and, when they do, they chant in unison, "I must, I must improve my bust."

Friday, 14 December

Fourteen weeks today. Our baby is the size of a fist and is growing downy hair, known as lanugo, across its entire body to protect the skin. The hair insulates the skin because there is a lack of fat. We are the proud creators of a fist-sized Yeti.

And it shows. For the first time, I noticed the bump through my wife's clothes. The sudden growth was the cause for much dancing around the living room and the onset of waddling. My wife has started to waddle. She feels the waddling is necessary, an easier way to carry the increasing weight below her belly button. I pointed out, rather tactlessly on hindsight, that she's boasted bigger bellies after a curry. We both know that the waddling accentuates the bump and triggers the occasional knowing smile from sympathetic mothers in supermarket queues. Nevertheless, my wife told me to bugger off before she waddled off to the bathroom to examine her bump again. I'm living in a scene from *March of the Penguins*.

Saturday, 15 December

We spent the afternoon playing the name game. Whenever prospective parents throw up name possibilities, one of them will invariably say, "Ooh, no, we can't call the kid 'Neil'. I once knew another kid called Neil. He was a sarcastic little bastard." This is why you won't find an Adolf born to a sane family anywhere since the fall of Berlin. We have all encountered a handful of brats who have thoroughly convinced us that we could never force their given name upon our innocent unborn child. However, my wife and I have an additional problem. She is a preschool teacher and there's probably not a name in the English language that she hasn't screamed across the classroom as the offending child buried the class pet hamster in the sandpit. The options for our firstborn are negligible.

"I like the older names," I began. "Good, old proper names like Charlie."

"Oh, I don't know about Charlie," my wife cautioned. "I once taught a Charlie in Singapore. He used to pull down his shorts to look at his little fishy."

"What about Billy then?"

"Yeah, I like Billy. No, wait … There was a Billy in England who painted a face on the back of my skirt."

"How about Harry?"

"Had a Harry in Singapore. His face was always covered in snot."

"Stanley?"

"He ate chalk."

"Well, what about girls' names then? How about Isabel?"

"Nope. Had one in Singapore. She used to throw shoes at all the boys' heads."

"Rosie then … Rosie's all right, surely. It's my nan's name. Let's have a Rosie after my nan."

"Nah, I had a Rosie in Australia. She couldn't stop farting."

"We'll keep her off the Brussels sprouts then."

Irritated by my wife's rejection of all my rational suggestions, I petulantly offered puerile word associations to all her name proposals.

"Let's try a few different names," she said. "What have been some of the newer names I've heard in class recently? … Ah, how about Indiana?"

"Jones."

"I've got a Ned."

"Kelly."

"I've had a Noah."

"The animals went in two by two, hurrah, hurrah."

"Ah, here's an unusual one I taught in Australia. How about Darcy?"

"Darcy? Are you serious? Will we pack him off to school in breeches, silver buckles and frilly collars and cuffs? Bloody Darcy indeed."

We were getting nowhere. For all parents, picking names is an extremely serious business, even though we desperately pretend that it's anything but. When Australian parents forgo Kylie and Brad for Darcy, it is a clear, transparent attempt to show that they are cool, laid-back, literate parents. These are parents who know their *Pride and Prejudice* from their *Sense and Sensibility*; their Colin Firth from their Hugh Grant. But they are living in a Jane Austen novel. In the real world, they will send their five-year-old to a no-nonsense, state-funded kindergarten with a name that belongs to a nineteenth-century upper-class fop. Shackle a kid with a name like Darcy and he may spend a considerable portion of his teenage years with his head down the toilet.

Selecting a child's name is also a precarious business. Get it oh-so-right now and it'll be oh-so-wrong tomorrow. In the fickle world of glossy magazines and trashy TV, the Scarletts and Kieras of today soon become the Britneys and Parises of yesterday. In 1974, my mother named me after Neil Young, the trendy song-writing activist. She adored his No.1 hit "Heart of Gold". In the 1970s, it was cool to be Neil. He was an astronaut (Armstrong) and he was a singer (Young, Diamond and yes, all right, Sedaka). In 1982, as I tried to make my way in a new Dagenham primary school, the BBC launched a punkish, anarchic new comedy called *The Young Ones*. Written by Ben Elton, the programme revolutionised the staid format of British comedy. It was must-see

TV and had cult classic stamped all over its irreverent, right-on scripts. Unfortunately for me, though, one of its most popular characters was a gangly, long-haired, lentil-eating, flared-trouser-wearing hippy called Neil. He was the village idiot of the 1980s. If you were guilty of moronic behaviour or if you were the office comic or the class clown, you were Neil. Well, I *was* Neil. It was my name. So according to the profound reasoning of my prepubescent classmates, I was a long-haired, lentil-eating, flared-trouser-wearing hippy. From about 1982 until 1985, the name Adolf Humphreys didn't seem like a bad alternative.

I was a wanker until secondary school when I met a real wanker. Or a Wayne Kerr to be more precise. Oh yes. There was a boy at secondary school whose parents—the Kerrs— thought it most acceptable to name their son Wayne. Wayne Kerr. Twelve years later, they packed him off to a Greater London comprehensive school, an institution where a boy with an amusing name is sure to escape ridicule.

Determined to steer well away from the fickleness of popular culture, I favour going back to the traditional and sticking with the tried and tested. For years now, I've favoured a Billy, Charlie or Harry running around the living room. The trouble is, so does everybody else. In the list of top 100 baby names in the UK in 2007, Jack sat proudly at the boys' summit for the thirteenth year in a row. Grace was the preferred choice for baby girls. You just can't get any more traditional than Jack and Grace. They go together like beanstalks and amazing anti-slavery hymns. Quirky is out, traditional is clearly back in. Indeed my favourite names—Harry, Charlie and Billy (William)—were all in the top ten. While Ella, the only girl's name that my wife and I occasionally agree on, also made the top ten for girls, along with the usual Brontë-like fare such as Emily, Lily and Olivia. I'm a sucker for tradition, but no one wants to be common.

Having dissected various top 100 baby name lists, we find ourselves in a bind. We love the Billys, Charlies and Harrys but are less keen on our child being known as "The Other Billy" or the "No, Not You, Charlie" in the classroom. As my wife keeps pointing out, teachers have the inevitable habit of classifying kids who have the same name. Families are no different. There are three Garys in my immediate family. For that reason alone, none of them can ever be called just Gary. They are Uncle Gary, Stepdad Gary and Brother Gary. Poor Brother Gary will spend the rest of his life sounding like he belongs in a monastery. We could end up with Loud Harry, Ginger Harry or Cousin Harry Who Eats His Own Hair. You never can tell. Notice I keep picking out names for boys. We cannot even agree on a name for a girl.

As a joke, my wife and I suggested calling our baby Dagenham, regardless of whether it's a boy or a girl, after our English hometown. If it was good enough for Brooklyn and the Beckhams, then it's good enough for us. Unlike Brooklyn however, Dagenham doesn't fare well in pop culture references. Peter Cook and Dudley Moore referenced the town in "The Dagenham Dialogues of Pete and Dud" (Moore grew up there. He went to the same school as my wife and me, a few decades earlier of course). Morrissey also wrote a half-baked satirical song on the place called "Dagenham Dave". Needless to say, that name was eventually vetoed.

We really do not want the baby sounding like a Wayne Kerr.

Sunday, 16 December

My poor wife's erratic hormones took their toll today. We were invited over to our neighbour's house for the annual Christmas get-together. I couldn't attend because I was working. This made my wife cry. She decided to make a trifle, but then realised she did not have all the ingredients. This made my wife cry. When she returned with the ingredients and pottered around the kitchen, I contributed by dancing around the kitchen while making up some daft limericks about getting an eyeful of trifle because I shot it with a rifle. This made my wife cry. I apologised for the appalling silly verses, made her stop everything and cuddled her. She rambled on about needing to cut up the Swiss rolls but I refused to let go. This made my wife cry. I also noticed though that she was starting to giggle through the tears. I pointed at the mixing bowl and insisted it was a trifling matter. She told me to fuck off. That was a good sign.

Monday, 17 December

Thank heavens for cocoa butter. As her belly continues to swell, my wife has been scratching like a flea-ravaged dog. Lately, her skin has been stretching considerably, which apparently makes the skin itchy, so she's been attacking it with her jagged fingernails. The friction sounds like sandpaper on a cactus. It's ever so attractive. Her antics remind me of those stray dogs who happily lie back to reveal a saggy pair of testicles to passers-by. They scratch their balls in a rhythmic fashion that is so utterly bewildering, it can be strangely hypnotic. A similar image confronts me on the sofa most evenings. My wife rips at her expanding flesh like a pack of hyenas devouring a wildebeest carcass. And it's contagious. As my wife collects layers of skin under her fingernails, I find myself rubbing my back up and down the back of the sofa and fidgeting with even more irritating regularity than usual.

Fortunately, a teaching colleague introduced my wife to the soothing benefits of a cocoa butter moisturising stick this evening. This product is priceless. Every pregnant woman's home should have one. Cocoa butter increases the elasticity of the skin and reduces that itchy, stretching sensation. I can no longer contemplate life without it. My wife has spent much of the night guiding the cocoa butter stick across her rising stomach in fussy, straight lines, rather like a groundsman's lawnmower at Wembley. At the end of each line, she lets out a strange, semi-erotic groan of pleasure. It's not good. I can't get a thing done.

Thursday, 20 December

An old mate has become my temporary parental role model. An older father, he is making a conscious decision not to make his son's social decisions for him. That's not as easy as it sounds. Without getting too sidetracked by the nature-nurture debate, I do loosely subscribe to the Jesuit motto "Give me a child until he is seven and I will show you the man." I'm not a student of Jesuit teachings, just a massive fan of the groundbreaking, socio-economic *Seven Up!* documentary (my mother and uncle can be seen in the background in the first episode!). By the age of seven, my first love was football. I supported West Ham and Billy Bonds was my favourite player. I also listened to John Lennon's music. My father's first love is football. He supports the Hammers and Bonds was his favourite player in the late 1970s. And I can still remember my mother's revulsion when Lennon was shot. Did I support West Ham because they were my local team or because my father did? The decision certainly wasn't based on merit. The Hammers were shit at the time.

Did I play football because it was my favourite sport, the national game or because I would have something to talk about with my once-a-week father after my parents divorced? I honestly cannot answer that question. My father never held a gun to my head when it came to my leisure pursuits, but it's true that we would have been stuck for conversation on Sunday afternoons if I'd taken up kayaking instead. Today, we still discuss the flagging fortunes of the Hammers but, fortunately, football is not our only topic of conversation.

Prospective parents always bore anyone who will listen to their protestations that they will allow their children to stand on their own two feet, pursue their own interests and find their own pastimes and hobbies. I vividly recall my uncle, a dedicated and decent triathlete, insisting that his two sons should follow their own sporting paths. By their teens, they were both pounding the track as promising triathletes. My old mate in Singapore, a golf fanatic, continues to spend time and money on turning his daughter into the next Michelle Wie.

That won't happen to me, I tell myself. I won't cry myself to sleep at night if my child refuses to wear West Ham pyjamas and doesn't sing "I'm Forever Blowing Bubbles" as a lullaby. If our child grows up in Australia, dismisses the English Premier League as "shit Pommy soccer", takes up Aussie Rules, supports the Geelong Cats, dyes its hair blond, spends the weekends ripping it up on a surfboard at Torquay's Bells Beach and calls everyone "dude", I will not call my dad in despair.

As a kid, I was often on the receiving end of such blinkered behaviour. Not from my father, but from my mates' fathers. We called it "frustrated father syndrome". Or "frustrated footballer syndrome". You know the type. The dad "could have been a contender, Charlie" but because he became sidetracked raising his brood, he channels all his pent-up frustration into turning his child into a winner, whether his child likes it or not.

The frustrated father can be insufferable if his child takes up an individual sport. Heaven forbid, though, if he plays a team game, as his teammates are equally culpable if they stall the anointed one's fast track to sporting greatness.

I was a goalkeeper in a local under-12s football team. I conceded goals. I conceded lots of goals. And for that reason, I was the easiest of targets for the frustrated father's club that gathered on the touchline every Sunday morning to scream vitriolic abuse at skinny, freezing kids. There was one particularly grotesque father, called Robin, who was a frustrated footballer, coach and manager all wrapped into one obese frame. Oh, he was a little ray of sunshine to us, fresh-faced young boys. His much-maligned son spent half the match terrified to run within 50 metres of the ball for fear of actually touching it and the other half apologising to his teammates for his father's latest torrent of abuse. Robin always mounted a video camera—this was when they were only marginally smaller than a suitcase—onto a tripod at the halfway line and usually ordered a terrified younger relative to record proceedings so he could conduct a post-match analysis at the next training session to highlight publicly our numerous mistakes and weaknesses. Robin was not the manager. He wasn't even our coach. He was just a detestable father that the club couldn't get rid of because he'd paid his son's match fees for the season.

Robin bullied several youngsters at the football matches, but I was his favourite target. We both knew why. I was the only kid whose parents rarely attended the games. I was vulnerable. Robin was a wanker. Why did he verbally abuse me? Because he could.

I'm loath to tempt fate because the moment someone announces their plans for parenthood, a family elder always pipes up with, "When you've got kids of your own, you'll understand. All your big plans will go out of the window. You wait and see." And they are usually right. But I'm reasonably sure that I'll follow my mate's route to fatherhood on this one. If the baby beneath the bump eventually decides that synchronised swimming is the way to go, I'll be there with the nose clips. And if it does want to spend its weekends kicking a round or oval ball around with its mates, I'll be there to offer nothing but encouragement.

I know that.

Robin made the decision for me.

Friday, 21 December

Fifteen weeks. The baby could have developed the habit of sucking its thumb by now, something my mother still does.

Today marked the worst day of the pregnancy and, for the sake of my hormonal wife's sanity, we cannot afford another like it.

The morning started brightly enough. A little apprehensive, we headed over to the local imaging unit for the nuchal translucency scan. This scan usually picks out any abnormalities, such as heart defects or Down's Syndrome. Ever since I found out that my wife was pregnant, I was insistent on having this scan. Although abortion was not going to be an option, we've both always maintained that if there were going to be any complications, we would want to know about them as early in the pregnancy as possible so that we could plan accordingly. I had my reasons.

Thanks to some roadworks, an unexpected traffic jam and a lack of parking spaces, we turned up ten minutes late for our appointment. Judging by the disgusted look on the face of the receptionist, you would have thought that I'd broken into her house and stolen all her kids' Christmas presents.

"You'll have to wait for a gap now before we can squeeze you in," she said, as we were shepherded into a corner like a pair of disruptive pupils. We were nervous. We were doing this alone. Both our families were over 10,000 km away.

Eventually, the centre's sonographer granted us a few minutes of her invaluable time. Middle-aged and permanently tetchy, the sonographer beckoned my wife over to the bed, ignoring my presence completely.

"Is it all right if I come in too," I asked, still feeling every bit the disruptive pupil.

"I suppose so," was the terse reply. She didn't bother to look up, preferring instead to play with her jelly tube.

"Ah, thanks," I replied, and then jabbered away nervously. "I mean, I am her husband. I'm not some random passer-by who's sneaked in because I've got a fetish for ultrasound scans."

"I know that."

She didn't do humour. She didn't do eye contact either.

My wife pulled up her top and shuddered as the cold gel was squirted onto her bloated stomach. There had not been a sudden growth spurt; she'd thrown back a few glasses of water to aid the scanning process.

"What's your due date?" the sonographer grunted.

"It started off as 14 June but our obstetrician thinks it could be a little further along, so we're hoping to clarify the date at this scan."

"That means you're fifteen weeks, almost sixteen weeks," interjected the sonographer, betraying the first glimpse of any emotion. "You can't have this scan then."

"I'm sorry?" I piped up. "Why not?"

"The baby's too big now. The best time, well, the only time, really, for the nuchal translucency scan is between 11 and 13½ weeks. The real cut-off point is thirteen weeks and six days.

We're way past that now. The skin on the neck will be too thick."

"But we're here at the right time," I pointed out. "We haven't changed appointment dates or anything."

"Who fixed you up with this appointment time then?"

"Our obstetrician's staff."

"They've given you the wrong date. You can't have the scan now."

I had to leave the building. I had never experienced rage like it. This was not a date to collect a parcel or get my teeth polished. This was a date that would determine the future of an unborn child. Our child. And it had been fucked up by human error. Through negligence on the part of others and ignorance on mine (I had no idea when the nuchal translucency scan had to be carried out), my unborn child had been let down. I returned to the car shaking. Naturally, but unforgivably, I took my guilt and frustration out on the only other person who felt as shitty as I did.

"Why the hell didn't we know this scan had to be done by thirteen weeks?" I shouted, as we stood at the pedestrian crossing in the mid-morning drizzle. "Why the hell didn't we know something like that? The woman in there obviously thought we should have done."

"Look, it wasn't our fault. We didn't book the appointment."

"But that's it. We can't take the test now. We can't get confirmation one way or the other. You know I wanted this test and now we're in the bloody dark."

"Don't shout at me, all right. The obstetrician's office made the mistake. Don't you dare try and take it out on me."

And there we stood, like a couple of feral delinquents, poisoning the air with invective and verbally abusing each other on a damp, gloomy street. Neither of us had done anything wrong, but rational thinking had disappeared the moment I stormed out of the scanning centre. Our ignorance was eating away at both of us. Someone had to pay for this. Someone whose office was actually just a brisk walk from the scanning centre.

"Right, come on," I barked at my equally livid wife. "We're not standing here screaming at each other for nothing."

I grabbed my wife's hand and led her across the pedestrian crossing. She knew where I was going. She did not think it was a good idea.

"No, Neil, not now. Don't see him while we're angry."

"Fuck it. It's the best time to see him."

The startled reaction of the obstetrician's receptionist practically rendered words unnecessary. Clearly, we were not carol singers. My wife and I conducted a brief, non-verbal conversation with our eyes before concluding that I should do the talking on the proviso that I kept my temper.

"Hello, we're here to have a word with the doctor as soon as possible," I said, in a loud whisper that every other pregnant woman in the waiting room heard. Naturally, they pretended they couldn't hear me. I was invisible and each of them was evidently reading the most gripping article ever written in an old pregnancy magazine.

"I don't think you have an appointment ..." the receptionist muttered.

"No, we don't. But we need to sort out immediately why you guys gave us the wrong date for the nuchal translucency scan. It's too late to have the scan now and should our child have any abnormalities, we can't plan for them because we won't know about them until the baby's born. All because you guys gave us the wrong appointment date."

The other pregnant women in the room gave up all pretence of reading their magazines. They were hanging on my every word.

"I'll have a word with the doctor," the receptionist mumbled, making eye contact only with my wife. "Please take a seat."

Within minutes, Dr Derek had smoothly ushered us into a private room for a chat. Softly, he asked us to sit down and sympathised with our predicament.

"Obviously a mistake has been made on our side and we are truly sorry," he whispered. I believed him, but that didn't make it right. Not at that moment anyway.

"I appreciate that, doctor, we both do. But we're not going to lie to you either. We are extremely frustrated. I know it's paranoia and I know I'm probably being irrational but I wanted to take every precautionary test possible. I've wanted to do that since I was sixteen," I croaked.

My throat was drying up.

"When my sister and I were teenagers, a doctor advised us to check for mental and physical abnormalities when we had children. I know my sister did the necessary checks when she was expecting her three boys but now I can't do it for our baby."

I looked across at my wife. She was crying. I held her hand as the doctor left the room to get a box of tissues.

On 15 May 1991, Manchester United was leading Barcelona 2–1 in the European Cup Winners' Cup Final when the phone rang. Ross and I exchanged knowing glances. Ross was my best mate and could always be relied upon to pop up as a much-needed crux on emotional occasions such as births, marriages and deaths.

"That must be your stepdad," Ross said, clearly as excited as I was.

"Yeah, I wish they could have waited a bit longer. There's only ten minutes left."

It was a teenage attempt at flippancy but I was fooling no one. The butterflies were playing havoc with my stomach. I never did see the last ten minutes of the match and missed Alex Ferguson winning his first European trophy with United.

"Neil, it's me," came my emotional stepfather's voice down the line. "Your mum's had a boy."

"Has she? That's brilliant. I've got a baby brother. That's brilliant ... Ross, Ross, my mum had a boy."

"Yeah? Nice one."

"Is everything all right? Is mum all right?" I asked. It wasn't a reflex question, but a genuine concern. Mum was in her late thirties at the time and labour had been exhausting.

"Yeah, your mum's fine, Neil. Everything's fine, Neil," replied my stepdad. "Just got to sort a few things out. That's all."

Those few things took almost two months to sort out in hospital and my baby brother was forced to display the kind of human courage that often culminates with a shiny medal if demonstrated in Iraq. My brother's bravery took place in an incubator.

After a botched delivery and an emergency Caesarean section, he was born with hypoglycaemia (his sugar count was too low so he couldn't produce enough glucose, the brain's fuel). As a result, the lengthy, traumatic birth caused some neurological damage. There was no way my tiny brother was going home. Just hours after coming into this world, mother and baby were separated. My mother, too weary to even stand, stayed in the local maternity ward while my brother was sent to the Great Ormond Street Hospital for Children on the other side of London. At the time, we were told that it was Princess Diana's favourite hospital after one of the princes had been successfully treated there. At the time, we couldn't have given a shit.

Only parents, and particularly mothers, will understand the separation. The next day my mother discharged herself on the condition that she stayed in bed (she couldn't do anything else). She came home and cried with an intensity that was disturbing. The maternal instinct to protect a newborn had been taken away from her and my exhausted mother struggled with the sheer helplessness of her situation.

"Go with your stepdad and see my boy," she whimpered to me, as I sat at the end of her bed. "Go and keep them both company."

"But what about you?"

"I'll be fine. Your sister's here. Go and be with your little brother."

There was a sense of urgency in her voice. I had to see my baby brother now. My mother wanted her three boys to be together.

After a painfully silent journey on the train, my stepdad and I ventured into the intensive care unit of the world's most famous children's hospital.

My baby brother was cocooned in an incubator with tubes everywhere. I held his tiny hand as my stepdad made desperate, heartbreaking attempts to sound reassuring. His voice kept breaking. This big man had never spoken in this way to me before and he sounded fragile and vulnerable. That scared me just as much as all the tubes that were hanging out of my baby brother's body.

My resolute mother somehow made it to the hospital within the next 48 hours, ripping all sorts of painful stitching in the process, and stubbornly insisted on visiting daily after that. Her presence was certainly necessary as the complicated birth evolved into an ongoing nightmare that none of us could wake up from.

When the hospital stabilised the hypoglycaemia with a glucose drip, my brother contracted meningitis. Miraculously, he got over that. Being so weak and susceptible to all the other illnesses that permeate a children's ward, he was then struck down with pneumonia. Any one of these conditions could have finished him off. With indomitable resilience and displaying a lion's courage, he fought back from the pneumonia. He exceeded even the most positive predictions of some of the world's leading paediatricians who had informed us that if he survived, he would be blind, unable to talk and confined to a wheelchair. He is none of those things. Today, he is a typical teenager. He's an opinionated little bugger with more girls around him than Hugh Hefner.

The doctors never discovered why my brother's birth had had so many harrowing complications. I never forgot the resident paediatrician telling my mother that as he could not determine the medical triggers, it wouldn't hurt for her children to take the relevant ultrasound scans and tests when the time came. Just for peace of mind. Now that time had come and all we wanted was peace of mind. We could not prevent a night like that from happening to us, but we could at least be ready for it.

Even by his own lofty standards, Dr Derek surpassed himself. He said we had every right to be frustrated as it was a parent's instinct and prerogative to want to find out as much about the baby's welfare as was technologically possible. He pointed out that there were other avenues available to us, even at this late stage, and that he would guide us through them.

First, there was a blood test called maternal serum screening (or Bart's test or triple screen). Taken roughly between fifteen and twenty weeks, the test evaluates the risk of chromosome abnormalities and/or neural tube defects by measuring the level of alpha-fetoprotein (AFP), a protein produced by the developing baby, as well as the levels of hCG and estriol (two pregnancy hormones). High or low levels of these substances (or markers) in my wife's blood could indicate the risk of certain defects.

Second, there was a high-fangled (i.e. expensive) ultrasound scanning machine in a clinic in East Melbourne that, while not as conclusive as the thirteenth-week scan, could gauge the probability of any neural or physical abnormalities.

Within the hour, Dr Derek had patted my wife's arm several times and booked us an appointment at the East Melbourne clinic. My wife had also given a blood sample.

The day had been truly shitty, but thank God for Dr Derek.

Monday, 24 December

Sixteen weeks today. The revised date was the only interesting upshot of Friday's traumatic events. Both Dr Derek and the sonographer agreed that the baby was older than originally estimated and the due date has been moved forward a few days. In fact, the date has been revised a couple of times. For the sake of consistency, my wife and I have settled on today as an appropriate marker. It is Christmas Eve and our baby is sixteen weeks old today. Tomorrow should be our last Christmas together as a couple. Tomorrow is also the day we go public. No one in the family is going to top our Christmas present.

Tuesday, 25 December

Our Christmas morning was spent like any other except that we were unable to begin a sentence without fronting it with "Next year, …" Sentences like "Next year, we'll have three piles of presents", "Next year, we'll have a high chair at the Christmas table" and "Next year, we'll be sleep deprived right through the festive season."

My wife's biggest fear about this Christmas Day was having an unexpected bout of sickness. The nausea has subsided quite a bit over the last couple of weeks but it does rear its head now and again, suppressing her appetite. Feeling unwell on Christmas Day is one thing, but if my wife lacked the stomach to eat her roast dinner, it could be years before the baby is forgiven.

We got through the usual festivities without any unwanted interruptions. We opened our presents, made breakfast, watched the new DVDs, ate most of the roast dinner and then we waited impatiently. Although we enjoyed the day, there was a perceptible sense of killing time and keeping busy until it was a reasonable hour to wake up the other side of the planet. Our families were eleven hours behind in England. We hung on until 6 p.m. our time, which was 7 a.m. in England. That was long enough. They could sleep when they're dead.

My mother was first. She has always been the earliest riser in our families. I was unexpectedly anxious as I dialled the number and waited for her to answer. She was seconds away from hearing that she was about to become a grandmother again and that her firstborn was finally on his way to having his firstborn.

"Hello, it's me. Guess what?! ... Oh, hello, mate, it's you. Happy Christmas, mate. Is mum there? ... Is she? Really?"

I was crestfallen. For the first time in at least a dozen Christmases, my mother had decided to sleep in.

"Yeah, she's not been feeling too well," my bored teenage brother replied down the phone. "I can wake her up if you want."

"No, there's no need for that. I'll call back in an hour."

I gave her 30 minutes. The suspense was too much. This time she was up.

"Hello, mum? It's me. Merry Christmas."

"Merry Christmas, merry Christmas," replied my croaky mother. "Sorry, I wasn't up earlier, I've come down with a cold. You had a good day?"

"Yeah, great, great. Did you like all your presents?" I asked. This was the opening line of a speech that I'd been rehearsing in my head for a couple of months.

"I don't know. I haven't opened any of your presents yet."

She'd screwed up my speech already.

"Oh, right. I see. Well, what I was going to say was that even when you've opened your presents, there is still another one to come, but you can't have it yet."

"Fair enough."

Was she doing this on purpose?

"Yeah, we can't physically give it to you yet."

"OK, no problem. I'm sure these presents are fine."

Like blood out of a stone.

"We will give it to you. It's just that it doesn't come out until around six months from now."

"That's fine. I'll have it then."

For God's sake, mum, stop being so obtuse.

"It's already taken three months to prepare but you'll have to wait another six months."

"Here, what's he on about?" my puzzled mother called out to my brother. "It's only been three months so I've got to wait another six for my present?"

"Come on, mum, think about it," I heard my brother shout in the background. "What takes nine months?"

A dramatic pause followed that lasted a fortnight. I practically heard the cogs turn.

"Nine months ... nine months ... No, no, it can't be," my mum rambled as the penny eventually dropped and smacked her across the back of the head. "Nine months ... that means you two will ..."

"Yes, mum."

"Six months from now, you two will ..."

"Yes, mum."

"Argh!"

She screamed down the phone. Then she dropped it. After picking it up, she cried repeatedly, "They're having a baby. They're having a baby." This must have sounded like the final scene of a delayed nativity play to the neighbours. Then she dropped the phone again before breaking down and sobbing uncontrollably. From then on, any semblance of coherence was lost. I had no idea what she was saying but it was a passable impression of a newborn crying. Fortunately, I had my teenage brother on hand to translate. Their dialogue was fascinating.

Wailing mum: Cabalayahababee.

Bored brother: She can't believe you're having a baby.

Wailing mum: Hanadwayawadun, wayawasan.

Bored brother: She had no idea what you were building up to. She couldn't work out what you were saying.

Wailing mum: Wahaahah, hoohawayahoowoo.

Bored brother: She's very emotional.

Thanks to the wonders of modern technology, I sent my mother a photograph of the baby's ultrasound scan via our mobile phones. I heard her phone beep over the sobbing and nose blowing.

"Mum, go and check your mobile phone," I said. "Open up the text message."

"OK, wait there. I'll just open it … What is it? What's that? Oh, is it a … It's a … baahaawaa, boohooaah."

The rest of the conversation was conducted in sporadic English and an ancient Swahili tongue.

I then called my father. One of the quirks of having divorced parents is that much of the time is spent performing the same task twice: two different family gatherings, two sets of Christmas cards and presents and two different phone calls on birthdays. There has even been two different Christmas dinners over the years. Festive occasions often feel like Groundhog Day: same day, same salutations and expressions of gratitude, just different times and different voices. I'm not complaining. This particular conversation was worth repeating.

"Hello dad, it's Neil," I began, with a general gaiety in keeping with the occasion. "Just called to wish you a Merry Christmas and to tell you there's another grandchild on the way."

"Nah …"

"Yeah, dad. Honest."

"Nah …"

"Yep, straight up, dad. We're having a baby."

"Nah …"

"Yeah, the first Humphreys grandchild is on its way."

This was a rather obvious attempt to curry a father's favour as my sister's already delivered three wonderful boys but I'll clutch at whatever straws I can.

"That's bloody great news that. I'm over the moon," my father replied. "Well done, mate."

"Yep. We're almost four months gone now."

"Nah …"

The reaction of my wife's parents was nothing short of abnormal. My mother-in-law also cried. She was delighted that we had finally managed to call her with a "present" that wasn't anticlimactic. My father-in-law applauded my efforts, before adding, "It bloody took long enough. I'd almost given up on you."

His joking pricked my sensitive ego. My bruised masculinity suddenly needed a massage. Without thinking, I divulged the relevant dates, from the moment we made the all-important decision to the time everything was put on hold while my mother visited and the short period it then took for the two lines to pop up in the right window.

"Bloody hell," the future grandfather of my unborn child replied. "You two must have been going at it like rabbits from the moment your mum left the house."

Wednesday, 26 December

When I become a father, I will always buy my child Christmas presents complete with batteries. Here we are at the end of 2007 and toy manufacturers are still stamping their boxes "batteries not included". In twenty years, nothing has changed. When I was a kid, I was convinced that the pharmacist who ran the nearby chemist's was running a Christmas battery racket. Throughout the course of the year, the only time I ventured into the shop, with its harsh fluorescent lighting and soapy smell, was when I accompanied my mother to get her "woman's things". I had no idea what they were but they always came in a brown paper bag and I always got a whistle lollipop so I didn't mind.

Just before Christmas, he painted "all kinds of batteries sold" on the shop window with whitewash, and then he waited. His was the only shop for miles that stayed open over Christmas.

Consequently, his shop represented the only chance I had to ignite my *Star Wars* light sabre and whack my sister over the head with it. I'm sure that that pharmacist made more money on batteries in one day than he did on verruca socks all year round.

So, to my unborn child, here is a Christmas promise: I swear every gift you receive from your parents will include batteries or I will personally go down to the chemist's until I am no longer physically capable. And by then, I'll need a lot more from a pharmacist than just batteries.

Friday, 28 December

I've taken to kissing my wife's swelling belly. I have no idea if this is normal dad-to-be behaviour and haven't come across any other prospective fathers doing it; not in the supermarket anyway. My wife was snapping up next year's Christmas cards at half price when I had this overwhelming urge to squeeze her protruding stomach. As this was out of the question, I settled for a quick peck instead.

"What are you doing?" she asked. "You can't do that."

"Why not?"

"We're in a supermarket."

"It's all right. You're pregnant. They let you do anything in public when you're pregnant. It's like breastfeeding and stuff."

"How many pregnant women do you know who breastfeed?"

"Oh, you know what I mean … Give us a kiss."

And I chased her into the frozen food aisle with puckered lips.

I enjoy chasing my pregnant wife around the supermarket. I am happy to dance around the boundaries of accepted norms of social behaviour, whatever they are, at the best of times. I always have. I am a proud product of a more innocent age when kids played in the street until 4 a.m., front doors were left open and the local policeman battered your daughter with his truncheon whenever she dropped a sweetie wrapper.

Back then, kids were less constrained by social convention. We interacted with strangers and even played with them. When I was growing up, we never assumed that every man we came across was a paedophile. My mother was far more concerned about speeding Ford Cortinas than she ever was about dirty old men.

"If you're going to play footy at that park that's 27 miles from our house," she would say, "Mind that big road when you cross it. It's a dual carriageway and, remember, you're only nine."

By the time I had reached the park, there were already 25 other kids there who had turned up from the far-flung corners of Dagenham. One boy's dad always popped over and conducted impromptu coaching sessions and refereed our matches. His name was Billy and he was usually "happy to get away from her over the road" for a couple of hours. I never met "her over the road", but we did hear her voice when she screamed at Billy and his son to go home for dinner. Billy, a skinny guy with a moustache, didn't appear to have a job but he was an oracle of football knowledge and told us, on countless occasions, that he would have signed for West Ham United if he hadn't met "her over the road".

We loved Billy. Matches were never the same unless Billy was there to officiate and offer advice. We would kick a ball around and make small talk until Billy came over with his son. Occasionally, the rising sense of anticipation would be too much and one of us would be delegated to knock on his door. I often found myself standing on Billy's doorstep knocking on the front door to see if the 40-year-old unemployed occupant wanted to come out to play. There was no stranger danger. We had no one to be afraid of because no one was a stranger to us.

In Singapore, I often kicked a ball around with some of the kids who played underneath our apartment block. Occasionally, the kids turned up at my front door and asked me to come out to play. I had, in effect, become Billy, which I did not have a problem with, but modern society does.

"You're going to have to stop that now," my wife said, after I turned them away because I had some work to do.

"Why? We're only knocking a ball about."

"It's not that. You're too old and they're too young."

"Too old for what? We kick a football against a concrete wall for ten minutes."

"You know what I mean."

"We've got to have our own kid, and the sooner the better. Then I can play again."

I was being flippant, but I knew exactly what she meant then and I still do. The nanny state isn't overly keen on men being around children anymore. Don't you read the papers? Strange men are dangerous. If you're a daddy, then somehow you're socially acceptable. You're allowed to be around, and talk to, other children. If you're not a father, however, then modern society would rather you kept your distance. As I still was not a father in Singapore, it was in my best interests to step back.

To be honest, I'm not entirely sure what my reaction would be if my prepubescent child returns home one night and says a 40-year-old man joined in and took charge of the football match. He's probably a great bloke, a genuine football fan and a decent father, like Billy was. But what if he isn't?

Saturday, 29 December

We ended up discussing the accepted norms of behaviour around children again this evening. I was annoyed with myself for allowing an element of self-doubt to creep in. Decent blokes like Billy, either fathers themselves or not, could be found organising football and cricket matches up and down the country when I was growing up, and still do in Australia, so why should I doubt their integrity now and even hint at an ulterior, sinister motive? The nanny state and a sensationalised media rambling on about paedophiles lurking behind every banner headline have clouded my judgement. I felt as though I had become an intimidated product of my fear-mongering environment. I needed a second opinion.

"You know I like having a laugh with kids, right?" I asked my wife, as she sat on the sofa rubbing her belly. "And you say that I should remember that I can't act like a big kid everywhere?"

"Yeah, so? I need to pee again so I hope you're making a point."

"We both agree that kids are too pampered nowadays. You know, wrapped up in cotton wool and all that, right? But here's the thing. You remember I told you about Billy?"

"That dodgy old bugger who played football with you and your mates?"

"Exactly. Some of my best childhood memories are those football matches. But what would you do if our kid came home from football and said a Billy-type bloke had joined in?"

"I wouldn't be too keen, I suppose."

"Yeah, nor would I."

We sat in silence for a while. Then my wife smiled.

"You know what it is, don't you?" she said, getting up slowly. "You're not thinking like a child anymore. You're thinking like a parent."

That was true, I suppose. I've always been a kid in an adult beanpole's body, but my perception was starting to change, if only slightly.

"I can still play my *Star Wars* game with the neighbour's grandson though, right?"

"Yes, Neil."

"And I can still kiss your belly when I want?"

"Yes, Neil. But not in the supermarket."

She waddled off to the toilet and left me to bask in my newfound maturity. I was starting to think like a parent. Imagine that. But if she thinks I'm going to stop kissing her belly in the supermarket, she's got another thing coming.

Sunday, 30 December

My wife's parents arrived today from England to stay with us for the next three weeks. It was an emotional reunion at the airport. My father-in-law thanked me again, in person this time, for "going at it like a pair of rabbits".

Monday, 31 December

Seventeen weeks today. Fingerprints are forming now so it had better not break the law when it's older.

The biggest physical change this week has been my wife's breasts. They are huge. At breakfast this morning, my in-laws asked their daughter if she felt any different and there were two rather obvious changes staring at them. They turned to me and asked the same question. I kept quiet and ate my cornflakes. As conversation stoppers go, "Your daughter's got an enormous pair of knockers" is right up there.

"I have been peeing a lot more recently," my wife suddenly piped up.

"You're not kidding," I said, grateful for any sort of distraction. "Our days out are now planned around public toilets."

In the last few weeks, my wife's urination frequency has gone through the roof. Her kidneys are working harder during pregnancy to flush out the waste. To complicate matters, her bladder is playing mind games. Ordinarily, the pressure of a full bladder sends a signal to the brain—that delightful peeing urge—which acts as a reminder that if it is not emptied soon, there could be a need to splash cold water over the groin area to cover the offending wet patch.

Now my wife is pregnant, however, the pressure of her expanding uterus against the bladder forces her urine depot to send confusing messages to the brain. The bladder demands emptying when there's barely anything in it. These demands are usually issued when we're in a supermarket queue or five minutes into a movie at the cinema. Once or twice, my wife has returned to the living room from the bathroom, sat down for two minutes, promptly got up again and shouted, "For fuck's sake, I've only just been!"

Fortunately, my father-in-law had the answer to her urination complications.

"Just go if you've gotta go," he mumbled over a mouthful of bacon.

"Thanks, dad, I never thought of that."

"No, what I mean is, you don't have to rush around trying to find a public toilet. You can go anywhere when you're pregnant," he said, clearly pleased with his startling revelation. "It's the law."

"It's the law?" I suddenly interjected. "Pregnant women can pee anywhere?"

"Yep, by the side of the road, beside their car, anywhere. It's the law."

He was beginning to sound like Judge Dread.

"Anywhere in the world, dad?" my wife asked.

"Yes, I'm telling you, it's one of those universal laws. An international law, part of some international charter. Pregnant women can go whenever and wherever they like."

I wasn't convinced.

"So if she gets caught short while queuing up for petrol, she can whip down her trousers and have a slash beside the petrol pump?"

"Yep, it's the law. I mean you wouldn't do that obviously. But in theory, if you did, no policeman could arrest you."

My father-in-law was convinced so I later made a couple of curious enquiries on the Internet. When I typed in 'pregnant women and urine', the search engine popped up hundreds of websites that were all related to home pregnancy kits, urine infections and the risk of preeclampsia. None of them told me if my wife could pee by a pump in a petrol station. In desperation I typed in "can pregnant women pee in public?". To my surprise, the subject had popped up once or twice in online chat rooms. I seriously challenged the credibility of the chat rooms, though, when one of the contributors insisted that taxi drivers could legally pee in public if they kept one hand on the steering wheel. One particular posting, allegedly written by a British policeman, insisted that urinating in the street is always a crime, regardless of the circumstances. I'm inclined to agree with that.

In the evening, we sat at Corio Bay and watched Geelong's fireworks display usher in 2008. We all took turns rubbing my wife's belly and I kissed it as the last of the fireworks exploded in the starry night sky above our adopted home. This year should mark the birth of our first child. Farewell sleep-filled nights, weekend lie-ins and blemish-free walls and carpets. That was the year that was. Instead, bring on a year of sleep depravation, vomit-stained shoulders and paint-stripping, smelly nappies.

It's coming. This is it. Don't get scared now.

Tuesday, 1 January 2008

We witnessed a bizarre incident in the early hours, a random act of violence that left me thinking about my unborn child's future. I'm no prude and I'm certainly no stranger to violence. Growing up on a council estate in Dagenham, I was mugged twice, witnessed a close friend get smashed over the head with a bottle and lost another mate when he was beaten to death at a nightclub. I escaped that clichéd aspect of working-class living by travelling to the other side of the planet. With my wife carrying our child, I'm not overly keen to return to it now.

Long after the last glittering rocket had exploded over Corio Bay to usher in 2008, my wife needed to use the toilet again. No surprises there. The four of us (plus the bladder-pushing bump) meandered along Geelong's waterfront. The evening was balmy and lots of families were enjoying the cooler breeze by the seafront. We found the toilets and my wife waddled off inside, closely followed by my mother-in-law.

My father-in-law and I stood outside the toilets, discussing the insufferable heat when a Neanderthal gang stopped for a swearing session across the road. They kicked off with a contest to see who knew the most swear words and who could shout them the loudest. Even though they drunkenly sprayed invective around the street, they were generally harmless until one drunk pushed another. It's always the scrawniest one, the most intoxicated one, the close-cropped one with a face like a smacked arse. Stripped to the waist, he squared up to one of the gang. His belligerent posture said "hard man" but his scrawny physique said "charity appeal".

Skinny Man pushed his opponent but his opponent was reluctant to take on someone who was less compos mentis than he was, quite a reasoned analysis for a guy who was dribbling. All dressed down and no one to punch, Skinny Man overcame his confusion by pushing anyone who crossed his path. Half the town had just gathered around the bay to watch the fireworks display so he had a lot of unwilling volunteers to push. Finally, inevitably, one of his fellow Neanderthals pushed him back, lighting the powder keg and triggering the night's real fireworks.

"You fucking wanker," Skinny Man shouted, still playing the swearing game, and pushed his opponent hard into the fence behind.

Then the beer bottle appeared. With tedious predictability, it was smashed across the top of the startled drunk's head. As the glass shattered and rained down on the pavement, parents moved quickly to shield their children, guiding them across the other side of the street to where we were standing. This is Australia. In the summer, kids and teenagers will wear shoes for school, weddings and funerals, but that's about it. Some of the children were barefoot and there was glass everywhere.

The girls in the group suddenly piped up. Whether one of them was Skinny Man's girlfriend or the partner of the guy who had been bottled, I couldn't say, but they screamed at each other with a feral ferocity that belonged in the Serengeti. Defending their wounded tribesmen, these girls spat out the usual "fucks" and "wankers", but with an aggression that wasn't so much scary as it was depressing. No one in the group looked older than sixteen. No one in the group ran away from the crime scene. No one appeared particularly afraid of the consequences of their actions and the Pink Ladies in the group were a hair's breadth away from instigating a riot. None of them gave a shit.

"It happens everywhere," my father-in-law sighed.

"Doesn't make it right though, does it? Their parents probably don't even know where they are, never mind that they're whacking lumps out of each other."

"No, I know, but what are you gonna do?"

I didn't know the answer. Nature, nurture, what difference does it make? If we're all Hobbesian brutes capable of beating the shit out of each other in front of horrified families at a communal fireworks display, what chance does my baby have? I know it's not the smartest move to be a new father and a misanthrope, but I am utterly terrified. Like my father-in-law said, what am I going to do when the time comes? If I'm lucky, I've got maybe twelve to fifteen years to find an answer. At this stage, I haven't got a clue.

Thursday, 3 January

The clinic's results for the maternal serum screening turned up in the mail today. There is little risk of a chromosome abnormality. That's stage one out of the way. Stage two—the decisive stage—is tomorrow.

Friday, 4 January

We took the train to East Melbourne. We had enough to worry about without being preoccupied with traffic jams and exorbitant parking fees. The ultrasound clinic had a plush carpet and cable TV in its waiting room, reminding patients that this was not a routine visit to the local GP and that all major credit cards were accepted.

Airing on the TV was a lifestyle documentary about a British gay couple who had given up their successful, corporate careers to buy a heritage-listed pub in an idyllic English village. The documentary followed their path towards first-time publicans and it was a welcome distraction, particularly the couple's thick black beards. They were tearfully explaining that their parents had thrown their life savings into the venture when we were called in to see the sonographer. I never did find out if the gay couple's pub was a hit or not. It still bugs me.

The affable doctor invited us into his luxurious surgery, which was bigger than the first flat we had rented in Singapore. Clearly from Southeast Asia but educated in the West, the Chinese chap had a wonderful accent that flitted from the crushingly narrow vowels of wealthy English counties to the longer, slightly nasal vowels of his homeland. I liked him immediately.

On a flat-screen TV, our baby's flickering image quickly appeared through the snow. The doctor certainly knew his way around a womb. Within moments, he had manoeuvred his little transducer into position behind the baby's reed-like neck.

"In this test, we're after the skin fold at the back of the neck," he said, with all the authority of a man who's been examining wombs with a view for years. "That's what we'd like to try to measure. As you know, it's not as good now as a predictor. Eleven to thirteen weeks is the best time. But from what I can see … at this stage … is that the skin fold is normal. The measurement of 4.3 mm is normal."

My wife and I glanced across at each other and smiled. The relief was palpable. The measurement of 4.3 mm seemed ridiculously thin and fragile to me, less than the width of a pencil, but the man with the scan appeared satisfied.

"I can tell you are both from England," he said brightly, as he measured both sides of the baby's brain.

"Yeah, we are originally," I replied, before adding proudly, "but we lived in Singapore for ten years before we came to Australia."

"Singapore? Really? I come from Kuching but I lived and worked in Hampshire for many, many years, you know."

The tiniest, tightest vowel on "know" gave that away. His adorable accent was almost royal-like.

"Well, I am happy to say that having looked at your baby, I haven't seen any signs to indicate any physical or neural abnormalities," he declared. "That doesn't exclude the possibility, remember. It just says the risk isn't high."

"That's good enough for me, doc," I replied chirpily, surprised by my own jovial familiarity with the man from Malaysia. "You've done a grand job."

"Let's see if we can get you a couple of nice scan photos."

The doctor dragged the transducer across my wife's belly and a ghostly image of our baby's face greeted us on the screen. Hollowed out and practically skeletal, it was nonetheless staring straight at us. Our baby was looking at us for the first time. The eyes and nose sockets were easily identifiable and the mouth appeared to be wide open. It was a sublime moment. For the first time, the blatantly obvious became clear to us both. We were the parents of the hooded villain from the *Scream* movies. Whatever else happens, our baby has a future modelling for Edvard Munch prints.

We didn't set foot on the plush carpet after the consultation. We floated out of the clinic. While we waited for the lift, we danced a little Native American-like jig in a circle repeatedly, which startled the middle-aged woman who stepped out of the lift moments later. We didn't care. In fact, we danced and giggled all the way home.

Sunday, 6 January

The Flintstones are running around my wife's belly. That was the most incisive description she could come up with for today's unexpected internal developments. The flutterings have begun.

"Doesn't it feel like balletic butterflies dancing around in your stomach?" I wondered, in a pathetic attempt to add some gravitas to this historic moment.

"Nope, it definitely feels like *The Flintstones*. Loads of bare feet scampering around below my belly button. Loads of little Flintstone legs."

That's marvellous. We're going to give birth to Barney Rubble.

The top of the uterus is now pushing itself upwards at an impressive rate and should be halfway between the pubic bone and the navel to make more space for little Barney. Our baby can literally stretch its legs now, around the eighteen-week mark, and the first sensations generally feel fluttery. This is the first physical connection between mother and baby, a gentle, barely perceptible, touching sensation. Like a butterfly on the hand. Thanks to my wife, I can only picture Fred Flintstone clubbing Wilma.

Unfortunately, this initial fluttering is not a spectator sport. We are still several weeks away from the punching and kicking. My involvement, sadly, is negligible. There were desperate, almost poignant, attempts on my wife's part to share in the moment.

"Quick, touch my belly now," she cried. "I can feel the flutterings."

I practically jumped on her stomach, feeling around and listening like a doctor with a stethoscope.

"There. There. I just felt another one. Move your hand over, mate."

"I did, but I can't feel anything. It's all internal. You can't feel anything externally either. It's inside."

"But that felt like a strong one ... There! There! Another one. Feel it?"

"No, mate. I can't feel the flutterings at this stage."

"Oh, you don't even care. Just go back to your bloody newspaper."

I can't wait for the baby to actually start kicking my wife. For several reasons.

Monday, 7 January

Eighteen weeks today. If it's a girl, she already has eggs of her own. I don't want my daughter having eggs of her own. I feel strangely indignant on the issue. The baby may also be able to hear now, too. Sound passes through bones to the inner ear, which should have hardened by now, while the area of the brain that processes nerve signals from the ears is also developing. My baby can hear. My baby can pick out my wife's voice and possibly those around her. My mother-in-law sat beside my wife on a plane for an hour this morning discussing a trashy magazine article that claimed a woman got her eyesight back thanks to her cat and the wonders of pet therapy. My poor, poor baby.

We took the in-laws on a short trip to Sydney today. On our last visit to the obstetrician, my wife checked if she could handle the one-hour flight. Dr Derek patted her arm and gave her the all-clear. He pointed out that it's not the flight itself that's the problem for pregnant women but the going into labour on a long-haul flight over the Pacific that tends to be a bit of a concern.

As we sat on the plane, my in-laws played the "you won't be able to" game. The object of this game was to irritate us as much as possible before we threw them out of the emergency exit somewhere over Canberra.

"You won't be able to do this when the baby comes along," my father-in-law pointed out. "You won't be able to fly anywhere."

"You won't be able to drive everywhere either," my mother-in-law interjected.

Clearly, we are going to lock ourselves and the baby in the pantry until it's sixteen.

"You won't be able to go to restaurants," my mother-in-law added, warming to her theme. "You won't be able to feed the baby and yourselves. No, you won't be able to eat anymore."

"You won't be able to sleep anymore," my father-in-law chimed in, clearly enjoying himself. "You won't be able to do anything once that baby comes along. Nothing at all."

We're thinking of locking ourselves in the pantry now.

Tuesday, 8 January

Everything has to be "loose-fitting". Walking along Sydney's George Street this afternoon, my wife's only concerns were finding "loose-fitting" garments and toilets. From the Rocks to Bondi Beach, there isn't a public facility in Sydney that my wife hasn't visited over the last 48 hours.

That evening, we had a "loose-fitting" fashion show back in our hotel room. The elastic waistbands practically sliced through my wife's armpits. She is an incontinent Simon Cowell.

Thursday, 10 January

Disciplining our child—or more pertinently how the discipline is administered—remains our uppermost concern. My father-in-law triggered another round of discussion today on our most popular topic by pointing out how Britain's anarchic monstrous youth is apparently impossible to control. My father-in-law paints a pretty grim picture of the English council estate I left behind. *Lord of the Flies* is not only a reality but the castaways have smashed the conch shell. Ralph is wearing a hoodie, calling everyone a "motherfucker", going out with a girl who can only say "whatever", leading the gang around the estate in a happy-slapping campaign and recording routine beatings on his mobile phone.

"You can't open the paper without reading about a stabbing or shooting," my father-in-law said over breakfast. "And a lot of them are carried out by kids."

"Yeah, it's terrible," I muttered, not really sure where the conversation was going.

"I blame the parents," he continued, before contradicting himself. "But they can't do anything now in England. You've got kids suing their parents because they've been smacked. It's all gone crazy."

The last time my mother hit me, she had to jump to make the necessary contact. I was 15 and lanky and my mother was 36 and shrinking. I can no longer recall my misdemeanour but I know that my teenage, hormonal angst offered plenty of reasons for regular discipline around that time. Shortly after my mother's jumping punch, I left home in a huff, vowing never to return. My stepdad waited an hour and then called me in from the back garden. My dinner was getting cold.

Parents hit kids when I was growing up in Dagenham. Almost all parents smacked their children. Working-class parents certainly did. It was practically a social pastime. They took their children to the supermarket and the beach to do it. Middle-class parents usually participated, although the broadsheet newspapers were beginning to frown upon this traditional form of discipline. The remaining kids at the top of the social pyramid were generally taken care of by the corporal punishment policies of their private schools.

Of course, parental discipline is evolving. We now live in enlightened times, establishing smack-free zones with a breathtaking sense of righteous superiority. We know better now. Our parents were ignorant. They didn't know how to raise children. They tried hard, bless them, but they were primitive. We've seen the error of our parents' ways and the fruits of our liberal, non-physical labours are there for all to see.

He's called a chav in Britain.

Or a bogan in Australia.

Or an *ah beng* in Singapore.

Now that's what I call enlightened parenting.

The chav. The bogan. The ah beng and his partner the *ah lien*. Call them whatever you like (no, really, call them whatever you like), but they are alive and most definitely kicking in all three countries that I have lived and worked in.

I've been to school with them. I've taught them. I've profited from them (they make for priceless material) and I've even been mugged by them. I'm just not too keen to live with them.

Part of the problem is that children are no longer disciplined with the same force or intensity as their parents', or even more so their grandparents', generation. I grew up after the generation who spoke fondly of strangers smacking them around the back of the head, teachers throwing chalk at them, headmasters caning them and parents hanging them in the living room. My parents' generation couldn't turn a street corner without stumbling across a line of people waiting to batter them.

I suppose a watered-down version of that domestic discipline was carried through to my generation. My mother did the smacking; my father did the finger pointing. My wife's parents did the same. It wasn't so much good cop, bad cop, as it was good parent, physically stronger parent. Until the age of ten, I required a stepladder to reach my father's waist. For him to knock me across the living room each time I forgot to record *Match of the Day* would have been a trifle unfair from a purely physical standpoint.

The argument for light smacking is straightforward. Children, particularly young children, respond to and remember sensations, including pain. I stick my hand in the fireplace. My mother smacks that hand. I remember the pain and associate it with sticking my hand in the fireplace. I decide not to stick my hand in the fireplace anymore. What could be simpler or more effective? If the smack was good enough for me and my wife, then, surely, it has to be good enough for our child.

In recent years, however, there has been a perceptible shift of opinion—smacking has become increasingly frowned upon. Whether the mood change can be attributed to the growing intervention of third parties (the media, social welfare groups, Oprah) or the general rise of the nanny state is a debate for another book. Regardless, children in my native country are now untouchable, literally and legally in some cases. In 2005, a radical law was passed allowing Westminster to take some control of every living room in the country. According to the law, parents in England and Wales who smacked their children so hard it left a mark would face up to five years in prison. To alleviate the growing suspicion that the nanny state was now all pervasive, a mind-blowing caveat was added. Mild smacking would be allowed under a "reasonable chastisement" defence against common assault. What constitutes "reasonable chastisement" and what counts as a mark? I left the occasional, temporary red mark on my little brother's arms as he cried with laughter while I blew fart noises on them. Does that make me guilty of child abuse?

On moral grounds, there is no counterargument. In the real world, however, the balance of power has shifted to the child—and the perceptive child knows this. He rules the classroom and reigns in the living room. If he tells you, his teacher, his parent or a social worker where to go, what can be done about it? No, really, what can be done about it? To hear my father-in-law discuss "kids today", you would think they all had horns sprouting beneath their hoodies. When did this fearless Hobbesian youth supposedly take control of Britain's streets? Maybe about the same time some well-meaning soul decided that the disciplinary techniques previously applied with considerable success throughout human history were no longer applicable in today's moral and just age. It is only a theory and not a particularly original one, but one certainly worth pondering the next time you worry about that spotty kid in the baseball cap standing behind you at the ATM.

Of course, I'm about to do a complete about-turn and contradict myself. I am not opposed to smacking a child as long as I do not have to do it. I'll happily play the jury, but not the judge. I'll gladly help determine if our child is guilty of sticking its fingers in a plug socket but my wife will be left to administer the discipline. I'm not trying to play the good cop here. I've already been saddled with the part of the heavy cop—I'm 1.94 m tall and weigh over 95 kg. My physicality leaves me with no choice. I will keep my hands to myself. It would be morally repugnant for me to strike a small child for, say, throwing some toys down the toilet. Of course, if it throws my *Star Wars* toys down the toilet, I'll put the bugger up for adoption.

If any light smacking is required, then I am hoping that my

wife will step in. I must emphasise that she's not entirely happy with this arrangement and it's by no means set in stone, but we are both proponents, and products, of the short, sharp shock. I will be on hand with the raised voice and steely-eyed glare. I hope it will be enough.

"It worked for you," I said to my sceptical father-in-law. "One fierce look from you and she'd behave immediately."

He laughed.

"She was a cheeky little sod. She got away with murder."

We all laughed because this was blatantly untrue.

"You obviously did a good job with her," I continued, determined to end the discipline discussion on an upbeat note.

He smiled ruefully.

"It's all changed now," he muttered. "Kids just don't have the same respect anymore. Not for each other. Not for their parents. No one."

The resignation in his voice stayed with me for the rest of the day. We have ideas about discipline, but that's all they are. Ideas. I don't have the answers. No parent does. Parenting books claim they do but our baby won't grow up in a book, it'll grow up in our living room.

What will I do if my child squares up to me in that living room fifteen years from now and tells me to fuck off? What *can* I do?

Saturday, 12 January

On a more positive note, we went baby shopping for the first time today. My in-laws were eager to buy something for the baby's nursery. As I opened the door to a baby shop, my wife dashed in and headed straight for the counter.

"Sorry to bother you," she said breathlessly. "But have you ..."

"It's straight through that door and first on the left," interjected the smiling shop assistant.

With one leg wrapped around the other, my wife hopped away. I was impressed.

"Excuse me, how did you know ..."

"If we didn't have a toilet in this place, we'd be mopping up puddles all day.

"So you often get women ..."

"Every single day. The moment they burst through, I know what they're after."

She was a lovely, bubbly woman, much like a favourite auntie, but she had an irksome habit of answering my questions before I'd even finished asking them.

On an earlier reconnaissance mission, my wife and in-laws had checked out this place to pick out a pram. They had narrowed their search down to two prime suspects and I was summoned this morning to help make a final decision. One was a good, old-fashioned pram—the sort I bounced around the streets of London in. High and wide, with frilly edges and a shiny silver frame, the pram was more of a stage for the baby to perform its cute cooing routine in public than it was a mode of transport. The pram was also expensive. The other one was less aesthetically pleasing, but stunningly practical. A three-in-one buggy, the carrycot could be removed with a couple of clicks. The chassis was pretty much the same as a standard pram but the seat faced towards the parents, which seemed more suitable (and safe) for newborns. Best of all, the carrycot could also be clicked into a base in the back seat and, hey presto, we had a car seat. The three-in-one was also on special offer and far cheaper than the fancy pram with all the bells and whistles. It's not difficult to see which way I was leaning. Our only concern—don't laugh if you're already a parent—was how protracted and complicated the process of attaching and removing the carrycot and opening and closing the buggy would be. I was on hand to play the role of crash test dummy using the shop's display model. If I ticked all the boxes without the baby being decapitated or harmed in any way (a doll was used as a substitute), we'd plump for the three-in-one.

My father-in-law, a grandfather, an experienced bus driver and a decent mechanic, was called upon to demonstrate how easy it was to open up the buggy and attach the carrycot. He couldn't do it.

The buggy went up and down on several, entertaining occasions but failed to stay in either position. After several ups and downs in quick succession, my father-in-law began to resemble an accordion player. He appeared to mumble a tune, too, but the only discernible lyrics were "fucking stupid thing".

"Are you OK over there?" the woman behind the counter called out. "Do you want me to show you how to put the buggy together?"

"We'll be fine," my father-in-law called back, with a forceful sense of finality. He has stripped down and restored motorbikes and steered double-decker buses around the tightest corners of central London. He knew what the woman could do with her offer of assistance.

"Let Neil try and do it," my mother-in-law suggested. "He's going to have to learn anyway."

My father let out a hollow laugh. Even my wife sniggered.

"Yeah. Go on, Neil," my wife said, clearly wishing the shop offered a comfy chair and some popcorn so that she could really enjoy the show.

Well, I put the damn thing together first time. Sorry, I know you were looking for a punchline. I know my family was. But I had my baby's buggy up in no time, with the carrycot clicked into place and reclined to the appropriate position so the doll faced me, hood pulled down and doll tucked in safely inside. A couple of clicks later and the carrycot was out of the buggy and attached to the car seat base. The doll didn't move once. My father-in-law was suitably unmoved.

"Lucky bastard," he whispered. Then he turned away and smiled.

Monday, 14 January

Nineteen weeks today. If all is progressing at the appropriate speed, our baby's eyes are now looking forward rather than to the side, which will certainly come in useful when it gets its first bike for Christmas.

Do not underestimate the importance of this physical development. Just a couple of days ago, we were admiring pelicans fighting for the scraps from some fishermen off the Queenscliff coast when my mother-in-law walked into a no parking sign. The collision made that comical clonk noise, ensuring that the rest of us couldn't walk for the next five minutes. We knew we shouldn't have laughed. We knew we were guilty of infantile behaviour. The poor woman smacked the sign so hard, the impact brought tears to her eyes. That just made it all the funnier. She insisted that she was looking down at the ground at the time. Well, that was a tremendous relief. For a moment, I had thought she was looking up, saw the sign but decided to headbutt it anyway.

My wife has inherited her mother's clumsiness and general lack of spatial awareness. She once slipped on our wet, tiled kitchen floor, forgetting that she herself had mopped it just five minutes earlier. So the genetic bumbling is a concern.

Tuesday, 15 January

My father-in-law's theory about pregnant women and urination laws was tested today. We took the in-laws to an idyllic little spot along the Great Ocean Road called Kennett River, a popular breeding ground for koalas. My mother-in-law had insisted that she was not returning to England until she had cuddled a wild koala in its natural habitat. We gave her a pickaxe, a rope and a pair of climbing boots, pointed her in the direction of the nearest gum tree and wished her all the best.

We were fortunate enough to spot over a dozen koalas in the forks of the trees. We could even see some newborns poking out of their mothers' pouches, which triggered much tummy rubbing. Spurred on by our initial natural discoveries, we ventured a little further up into the magnificent Great Otway National Park to continue our koala hunt. There were more koalas, but there were fewer toilets. Well, there were no toilets.

"I've gotta go," my wife muttered, clutching her groin area as if her hand might somehow serve as a dam to hold back the impending torrent.

"You went just before we left," I pointed out. "That was only twenty minutes ago."

"Well, I need to go now. You three need to act as lookouts."

My wife struggles to navigate her car out of the driveway. When she needs to pee, she can organise, delegate, strategise and execute with the kind of focused efficiency not seen since Wellington at Waterloo.

"Right, dad. You go to the end of the road where it bends so that you can see any cars coming up," she barked, pointing towards the bend, which was some 200 m away.

"But that bend's almost ..."

"I need to pee, dad! Mum, you stand at the back of the car and keep an eye on anyone coming up in the opposite direction."

"Right, no problem. No one's getting past me," she said, clearly savouring the responsibility while marching off past the car.

"Neil, you open the car doors and I'll crouch between them. They'll block off both sides. Hurry up."

"That's brilliant," I replied, genuinely overawed by her spontaneity. "You don't know how to work the TV remote control but you can show militaristic ingenuity when you need to pee."

But she wasn't listening. She'd already dropped to the crouching position and was carrying out the operation. Tucked between two open car doors, she still directed proceedings.

"Anyone coming up your side, dad?" she bellowed down the road, drawing more attention than if we were all running through the forest naked.

"No."

"What about you, mum?"

"No, it's all quiet."

"Can you see anything, Neil?"

"Yeah, a dozen German backpackers whistling 'The Happy Wanderer'."

"Sod off."

When she finished, I wandered off into the foliage to go behind a tree. It's contagious, you know. Some people have sympathy pains for their partners. I have sympathy pees.

Friday, 18 January

An emotional day. Things kicked off with a lunchtime date with Dr Derek. Or at least it should have done. At the last moment, the obstetrician had to dash off to hospital to deliver a premature baby. They're damn inconsiderate, these pregnant women. The silver lining came in the form of a lovely, young midwife who invited our mob into her quaint little room.

The room was smaller than Dr Derek's, but with just as many photographs of him holding newborn babies. Even though he was currently stuck between a pair of legs and shouting "Push", his presence surrounded us. Always. He was Obi-Wan Kenobi.

We invited the in-laws along as a final treat before they headed off to Melbourne Airport and back to England's bleak midwinter. The ultrasound scan made my mother-in-law cry. They didn't have them in her day. Back then, our mothers went to the local GP, who poked their stomachs around for a bit, told them not to smoke more than twenty a day and sent them home on the bus with a couple of bottles of stout.

At the risk of sounding blasé, the ultrasound scan was a little underwhelming on this occasion. It had only been two weeks since we'd had the scan in East Melbourne, which had been state of the art and extremely important. The contrast was rather like watching the rebirth scene at the end of Kubrick's *2001: A Space Odyssey* at an IMAX cinema and then seeing it again, a fortnight later, on a grainy black-and-white portable TV. I certainly wasn't ungrateful though. I still enjoyed the experience, particularly picking out all the fingers. However, on a tiny screen where only the midwife could really identify most of the essential shapes and sizes, it was more for her benefit than for ours.

She weighed my wife, who still only came in at a dainty 51 kg, less than her prepregnancy weight. Her appetite suffered in the first, nauseous trimester and anything containing nutritional value that she managed to keep down went straight to the little one. She was the one who lost out. The midwife insisted that the weight loss was quite common, but it has created a fascinating physical contrast. From behind, my wife is now blessed with the kind of curves she hasn't had since she was 21. From the side, she looks like she's swallowed a rugby ball.

"Should I be worried about the weight?" my wife asked.

"No, your baby's taking in all the good stuff it needs," replied the upbeat midwife. "Are you eating plenty?"

"Not as much as I'd like, but I'm getting there."

"Well, you might want to think about some multi-vitamins, perhaps, but there is no issue with your weight."

So if you're on the slender side during pregnancy, but still eating reasonably regularly, do not panic. The baby gets all it needs. My wife was told she could discontinue the folic acid, which was a welcome relief. She still cuts Panadol tablets into quarters before swallowing them, one at a time, with a reservoir of water.

Taking after its father, the baby's length confounded medical science again and the due date was pushed forward, once again. This time to 4 June. Apparently, the baby's length and weight indicated that it was hurtling towards 21 weeks.

The midwife booked us in for the important twenty-week scan at the imaging centre, which would now be a week late. The story of this baby's life so far. She also told my wife that, if she could manage it, she should bring along a urine sample in a small jar to each monthly check-up from now on. Could she manage it? My wife could bring along monthly samples in a water tank.

Outside the doctor's surgery, my sniffing mother-in-law stopped to blow her nose and wipe her eyes.

"That was amazing, wasn't it?" she said, after a furious blow of such intensity that she checked the contents of her handkerchief (probably to see if her nasal septum was in it). "I've never seen one of those scans before."

My father-in-law cleared his throat, obviously preparing to utter something of considerable magnitude after witnessing the movements of his unborn grandchild for the first time.

"That was all right, weren't it?" he said.

Eight hours later and there were more tears. We stood outside the departure lounge at Melbourne Airport, hanging onto those last seconds as if they were going to somehow prevent the inevitable separation. My in-laws were leaving. If everything proceeds healthily, we should be parents the next time we meet at the airport. But for now, it was about saying goodbye, which has never been easy. In England, in Singapore and now in Australia, my wife and I have left our parents behind on God knows how many occasions. Saying goodbye to a daughter is difficult enough, but saying goodbye to a pregnant daughter is heartbreaking.

My father-in-law, who will gladly drive 200 metres past a bus stop before opening the doors if the passengers on board annoy him, was a different man now. He rubbed his daughter's belly and tearfully whispered goodbye to his unborn grandchild. Even I had to turn away. The scene was bloody awful. Then he hugged me and said, "Look after them both, mate."

My throat began to tighten. He'd never referred to his daughter as "them" before.

"Of course I will," I replied, in a misguided attempt at jauntiness that was betrayed by my croaky voice. "I don't know how to do anything else, do I?"

They lingered for a little longer to cuddle their daughter again and rub her belly one last time. Then they were gone and we were alone again. My mother visited last August and my in-laws had just left. They planned to return in mid-June and my mother was coming out in July.

The baby is due on 4 June. The three of us are on our own now.

Saturday, 19 January

The poignant image of my father-in-law rubbing his daughter's belly still lingers. Daughters break their fathers' hearts. Yes, I know a child of either sex can break both parents' hearts, but there is just something primitive in the protective relationship between father and daughter.

The mere prospect of being a father to a teenage girl is more than enough to keep me awake at night. When I first met my future in-laws, I admired their liberal parenting in allowing their daughter's boyfriend to sleep on the sofa in his loud, silver shirt and high waistband trousers. I applauded their rationale that if they granted their daughter enough trust, then she would reciprocate. What forward-thinking, rational, level-headed parents they were, I thought to myself as I made myself comfortable on the sofa to watch a late-night episode of *The Equalizer*. What do I think about it now? I am appalled by their foolhardiness and told them so while they were here.

"I can't believe you let me stay all those Saturday nights," I said one evening, during another lengthy conversation on parenting styles.

"Well, what else are you going to do?" my mother-in-law retorted. "It was obvious that you were both quite serious."

"I'm not allowing my daughter's boyfriends to stay over," I replied indignantly. "No bloody way."

My in-laws laughed.

"You'll see," my mother-in-law said.

"Yeah, I know. But I still have a suspicion that a daughter would break my heart."

"Ah, that's true," my father-in-law nodded ruefully. "That's very true."

There's nothing wrong with fathers having special relationships with their little girls. The trouble is, of course, that the closer the relationship, the more chance there is that it might become strained during adolescence. The very notion of my future daughter dressing up to look seductive or even sexy for a male makes me shudder. I know what teenage males are like. I know what they want. I used to go to school with lots of them. Their brains are in their balls and have you seen how small *they* are? If a teenage girl asks a teenage boy how his English lesson was, the answer is all too obvious—she wants to have sex with him. If she asks him for directions to the train station, she wants sex with him. If she asks him the time, she wants sex with him. Never underestimate the predictability of the teenage male.

I was no different. When I stepped out of my school uniform and into my own clothes and stayed on for A levels during Year 12, I was convinced I had been transformed overnight into a witty sex god. The shiny, always-slightly-too-short shell suit and far-too-bright white trainers only boosted my chances. Everyone wanted to have sex with me. It was, like, totally obvious.

"Here, Ross, you know that Tracy bird?" I'd shout across the common room to my best mate.

"Who? The one with the eyes?" he'd shout back, momentarily lifting his head above his copy of the *Sun*.

"Yeah. The one with the eyes. I just opened the door for her and she smiled."

"Yeah? I reckon you're well in there then."

"Definitely. She's gagging for it."

"Yeah, well, I'm gonna sort out that Kerry later."

"Are ya?"

"Yeah. I told her that joke about King Kong's balls and she pissed herself laughing so I'm gonna ask her out after lunch. I'll be shagging her this time next week."

"Nice one."

And we were considered to be two of the school's brighter students. We were the sort of clean-cut young boys that you'd be happy to take home to your mother, but I'm not keen on the prospect of my daughter bringing either home to her mother. If, sixteen years from now, I should find a Ross or a Neil lying on my sofa, I can't see me being as accommodating and understanding as my father-in-law.

The adolescent years will be tricky. I can only hope that my daughter's taste in hormonal teenagers will be influenced by me a little. I know dear old Sigmund Freud reinforced the belief that the mother-child bond was the only relationship really worth worrying about and I do have a close relationship with my own mum. But I also think Freud was talking bollocks. The way I treat the women in the house, both my wife and any daughters, will have a direct bearing on what my daughter deems acceptable behaviour for a man in her household. The same rationale applies for a son too, of course, but unless he is gay, he will not have to pick a man to live with. My daughter probably will. To use one of the more obvious examples, there is the cycle of violence argument and the belief that a number of women raised by violent fathers often end up in relationships with violent men. If such a wretched cycle is a result of paternal conditioning, then there is an even greater incentive to keep my hands off and leave any physical disciplining to my wife.

And that includes future boyfriends. I'm not naïve. If I kick a boyfriend out of the house, my tearful love-struck daughter will run after him. Should I even hint that her drug-smuggling, brothel-running, gun-toting, chicken-molesting boyfriend might not be the man of her dreams, she'll scream back that I don't understand true love. If I imply that she's going out dressed like a lap dancer, her self-esteem will disintegrate, the clothes will get racier, the eyeliner will get thicker and the lipstick brighter.

All I can do is be there. Freud's followers practically propagated the notion that fathers did little more for their daughters than provide the sperm, the salary and the occasional cry of "go and see your mother". I'm not having that. This parenting lark is a double act, not a one-woman band. I'll be on hand to offer advice when my daughter comes home with a lanky, loud bugger in an even louder shell suit. But he's still not sleeping on my sofa.

Sunday, 20 January

There was a reference in a newspaper today that certain episodes of *Sesame Street* are no longer suitable for young children. Can you believe it? The original Children's Television Workshop, a non-profit organisation established in the United States to produce popular shows like *Sesame Street*, has supposedly made some episodes that are dangerous for kids.

The fun police, the PC police or the "tut-tut" police—call them what you will—has recently slapped an "adults only" warning on a DVD compilation of classic episodes of *Sesame Street*, a programme that I used to love. So did my wife, who is a preschool teacher. So did my sister, who is a primary school teacher. But what do we, along with the rest of the sane world, know? *Sesame Street* is bad, man.

The episodes, produced between 1969 and 1974, were released on DVD in the United States with the warning: "These early *Sesame Street* episodes are intended for grown-ups and may not suit the needs of today's preschool child." I was born in 1974. I grew up watching those episodes. Of course, I will readily acknowledge that cultural sensitivities change, and usually for the better. I also grew up watching a London-based sitcom about migrant workers learning English called *Mind Your Language*, which might as well have been called *Mind Your Racism*. I'm sure there are some faux pas in those early *Sesame Street* episodes. I mean, some of the alarming scenes of hosts wearing billowing, flared trousers and spouting enormous sideburns might be too distressing for children on a flat-screen TV.

The real reasons for the fun police's DVD warning, however, were far more sinister. On children's TV back in the 1970s, children were spotted playing in the street. Shocking, I know. Some even enjoyed the experience. Many played in the street until dinner time without their parents informing the emergency services, the nearest social welfare department or Supernanny first. On *Sesame Street*, kids played together everywhere. They skipped together, played tag together, shared stories together, and all on the street. One can only begin to imagine how disadvantaged, disillusioned and marginalised they must feel in today's street-free society.

When they were not hanging out collectively on a street and refining their social skills, they were brushing up on the alphabet with a cookie-gorging monster. Oh, the horror of it all. He was blue, ate cookies and was a monster. Such a distorted slant on reality would be too much for today's well-adjusted child. You see, blue, cookie-eating monsters do not exist in the real world.

The Cookie Monster also presented dietary concerns. A children's character gorging on junk food was no longer deemed appropriate for the healthy child of the new millennium. Today, you cannot step into a secondary school without stumbling upon a teenager nibbling on a lettuce leaf or munching on a muesli bar, thanks to the sterling efforts of the fun police.

In *Sesame Street*'s fledgling days, Big Bird's dopey friend Mr Snuffleupagus, who has the second greatest name after my old English teacher Ms Shufflebottom, was still imaginary. He was Big Bird's imaginary friend but, you see, kids do not have imaginary friends anymore because they encourage "delusional behaviour". Kids have never encountered a 2-m tall, talking, yellow bird in tights before either, but Big Bird didn't trigger bouts of delusional behaviour.

Worst of all, the grumpy, trash-loving but truly magnificent Oscar the Grouch was collared for his persistent bad manners and debatable hygiene. He was bitchy, possessed an acerbic tongue and took no shit. He was everyone's favourite character in *Sesame Street*. Oscar the Grouch, the delightful grumpy old bastard that he is, still makes me laugh today. Am I out of touch with reality? Every kid knows a cantankerous old uncle or a crotchety grandparent like dear old Oscar.

Children are not stupid. They only run rings around us in the living room or the classroom when we assume that they are. Just as they can spot an incompetent teacher within moments of her walking nervously into the classroom, they can draw the line between fantasy and reality. By whitewashing early episodes of *Sesame Street*, the fun police are attempting to fabricate a sanitised world that does not exist in reality. That's far more dangerous than a green puppet telling kids to piss off once in a while.

I truly hope our child grows up with Big Bird, Mr Snuffleupagus, the Cookie Monster and especially Oscar the Grouch, the funniest puppet outside *The Muppet Show*. In fact, now I think of it, I might buy our baby that particular *Sesame Street* DVD for Christmas.

Monday, 21 January

21 weeks today. Thanks to the midwife's calculations and our baby's growth spurt, we have jumped a week. Meconium is now beginning to pile up in the baby's bowels. Resembling dark green/black goo, meconium is the baby's first stool. The tar-like stuff is a wonderful combination of amniotic fluid and digestive secretion. Our baby will store the meconium up in its intestines and should present it to us just after birth. In effect, this is the makings of our baby's first poo, a historic event to be sure.

We celebrated with a curry.

Wednesday, 23 January

We visited the hospital where our baby will come into the world for the first time today. While we were there, we signed up for some antenatal classes. However, they are not called antenatal classes anymore. They are now called Parent Education Programmes. Of course they are.

Thursday, 24 January

As the baby nears its 22nd week, we had the twenty-week ultrasound scan today. Our child will be late for its own birth at this rate. When we arrived at the imaging centre, the assiduous staff informed us that they were running behind schedule. This scan was already over a week late, so another 30 minutes wasn't going to make much difference. But the delay made a considerable difference to my wife. She was not allowed to go.

"I'm desperate for a pee," she hissed, as I got over the shock that Tom Cruise and Katie Holmes were expecting another baby.

"Have you read this magazine article? It says that …"

"Never mind that. If I don't go now, there's gonna be a puddle under this chair."

"You can't go. You know that. The midwife said you need a full bladder before these scans ... I can't believe Tom Cruise is having another kid so soon."

My wife ripped the magazine out of my hands.

"This magazine is two years old. You've got to stop reading women's magazines in these places. I'm going to pee all over this carpet right now."

"Mrs Humphreys?" the sonographer called out.

"Oh, hello, how are you?" my smiling, beguiling wife replied. "Ready when you are ... Yes, I'm fine, thanks. Looking forward to the scan."

She's got more faces than the town hall clock.

The twenty-week scan was worth the wait. On a wider, flat screen, our baby was not only clearly visible and had, for the first time, distinguishable physical features, but the not-so-little one also performed for its audience.

"Now it's rubbing its hands together," the sonographer pointed out. "Now it's lying on its back and wiggling its feet. And now it's flipped over again and appears to be clapping its hands."

This was a trip to Sea World. I had to stop myself from throwing dead fish at the screen. It was a glorious moment, truly one of the highlights of the pregnancy. Neither parent should miss the twenty-week scan. Instead, all parents-to-be should invite family members and charge admission.

"I hope you enjoyed that little show," the sonographer said. "Now, let's get down to business."

And she did, with effortless efficiency. My wife's cervix and placenta were examined first. Then it was the baby's turn.

Both sides of the brain, the back of the neck, the brain stem, the distance between the eyes, the spine and the kidneys were measured on screen. The detailed, methodical examination was remarkable. We were told that the baby was around 15 to 16 cm. Check those measurements on a ruler. Decent-sized bananas come in at a longer length. Yet here we were measuring the baby's kidneys and getting a close-up of its rapidly beating heart.

"All looks pretty good, doesn't it?" the sonographer said. "Let's take a 4-D look at the baby now, shall we?"

"Sure," we said, not having a clue what a 4-D scan was.

"Rather than showing 2-D black-and-white images, this scan shows you live action, in colour," she said, reading our minds.

"Ah, yeah, we'll have some of that," I replied excitedly.

Forget a Kodak moment. This would be the definitive Kubrick moment. Finally, the screen would recreate the final, and my favourite, scene in *2001: A Space Odyssey* in all its hypnotic glory with our baby as the Star Child.

Naturally, our baby suffered a sudden attack of stage fright. The moment the sonographer switched over to 4-D, the baby turned into a native marsupial and tucked its head away inside its own pouch.

The technology was extraordinary though. Similar to radar, low frequency sound waves were sent into the body and the returning echo generated the 4-D image. The image before us was of a pair of wobbly, skin-coloured elbows. That's all our shy baby was prepared to offer. The sonographer probed around my wife's belly, but the baby was always one step ahead, altering its position, ducking away, tilting its head or using its hands to shield itself from the spotlight. We felt like the paparazzi. I expected the 4-D scan to eventually capture our baby stepping out of a designer boutique, wearing dark shades and sipping a latte.

We did grab one beautiful image of the baby curled up peacefully in the foetal position, showing the delicate curvature of the spine, but of course it didn't last. The baby flipped, looked directly at the screen for a fleeting moment and then turned away again. As our teasing fidget moved so fast, we were presented with a distorted, fried egg-shaped face. The image will never leave me. But then, the image of John Hurt playing *The Elephant Man* will never leave me either.

"It looks like the elephant man, doesn't it?" I said, as we strolled back to the car examining the photos from the scan.

"Don't be horrible," replied my wife, obviously hurt by the Hurt reference.

"I'm not. I'm only messing about. Besides, I always wanted our child to look like a movie star."

And with that, I hobbled off down the street shouting, "My name is John Merrick! I am not an animal!"

Monday, 28 January

22 weeks today. The bump is really taking off and my wife has taken to putting her hands behind her hips at every opportunity. She says it's comfortable. I say she's pushing out the bump for the neighbours' benefit. She still isn't gaining weight anywhere else though. I know most pregnant women would give anything to escape the chubby ankles, fingers, wrists and thighs and I also know that the baby will take all the nutrients it requires regardless of its mother's size and physique, but the baby is not my concern. My wife still hasn't reached her prepregnancy weight and if the baby takes after me, the voracious one will literally be eating her out of house and home. My wife is taking care of the baby's health but I don't feel I'm doing enough to take care of hers.

Tuesday, 29 January

We cannot have enough iron and calcium in the house. They are the bees in my bonnet. Preoccupied with my wife's weight, general well-being and our vegetarian diet, I checked a pregnant woman's dietary needs and, frankly, she cannot get enough iron and calcium down her gullet. Our pantry is a veritable forest now. It's like *FernGully* in there. You can't move for green leafy vegetables. We have so much spinach in its various guises that I may end up with enormous tattoo-covered biceps and shouting "that's all I can stands cuz I can't stands n'more" the next time I get caught in a traffic jam.

The fridge is piled up with yoghurts, dried fruit and litres of milk and my wife has already been heard muttering, "If I see one more bloody cornflake."

I think she is only joking, but I don't care. I have got to look after my old mate.

Wednesday, 30 January

My wife is at that socially delicate stage now where she has a bump, but it does not quite protrude enough to provide irrefutable proof that she's pregnant. She could just be fat.

Watching that uncertainty in others is delicious. You can see the conflict in their eyes. As those fleeting glances towards my wife's belly become more frequent and sustained, the indecision is self-evident. My wife looks pregnant. She's wearing those loose-fitting tops that pregnant women favour. She prefers the upturned hand pushed against the back of the hip and there is that conspicuous waddle popular with pregnant women. She must be pregnant. She has to be pregnant. She is pregnant. Having reached a definitive conclusion, they smile and take a couple of tentative steps towards my wife's stomach before stopping abruptly. She could just be fat.

The new school year kicked off this week and my wife welcomed 25 new kids to the class while their parents pondered this dilemma. Is my child's new teacher pregnant or is she fat? Pregnant or fat? Fat or pregnant? Pregnant or fat? Pregnant, fat, pregnant, fat, pregnant, fat ... forget it, I'll ask her teaching assistant.

The classroom assistant was collared over and over again by the cockatoo's cage, and each brief meeting was concluded with a cry of "I knew it!"

"I heard the good news," each parent whispered to my wife. "I thought I'd just check with your assistant first because you don't like to, you know, well, I didn't want you to think that I thought you were, you know. Well, you can't be sure, can you? And, well ... where should I put little Damien's lunchbox?"

The pregnancy dilemma has been marvellous. Watching friends and strangers tiptoe around the social taboo of obesity and a woman's waistline has been one of the high points. I must confess that I have taken the liberty of contributing to the discomfort of others. When someone has congratulated us, I have, on a couple of occasions, replied, "What for?"

"For the pregnancy."

"Why? Who's pregnant?"

I wait only long enough for *The Blair Witch Project* grimace of horror before acknowledging the truth.

Once the belly has been attributed to a foetus rather than too much Cadbury's, two things usually happen. First, there is the reflexive, and then swiftly aborted, tummy touch. Then I usually get reprimanded by the offender to mask their embarrassment. We visited one of our friends today to show off the bump and his hand instinctively moved to an area that is, remember, slightly above my wife's vagina. His intentions were honourable but, aside from lending each other the odd DVD, he realised he didn't know either of us well enough to be rubbing my wife's body parts. So he checked himself and guided his hand upwards to scratch his head. Smooth? He looked like C-3PO.

To deflect attention from the abrupt tummy touch withdrawal, he turned away from my wife and focused on me, giving me the diverting reprimand.

"You've got to look after this girl now," he said. "You shouldn't let her lift a finger around the house anymore."

"No, I've been trying to help where I can."

"You've got to," our friend continued. "You've got to make life easy for this girl from now on. She should be resting and you should be waiting on her hand and foot."

"Yeah, I do. We'll probably take it easy after we've been shopping."

"Shopping? She shouldn't be doing the shopping. You should be doing all of that now."

He had almost rubbed my wife's pubic area and I ended up on the receiving end of a public dressing down.

I'm finding other people's attitude towards my wife fascinating and—if I'm being honest—a little exasperating. Somehow, she has become public property. Subjects and behaviour that are usually deemed taboo or inappropriate are fair game for pregnant women. Relatives, friends, neighbours, medical practitioners and even strangers often mean well, but their tongues uncontrollably take off at the sight of a swollen bump. Weight, physical appearance, diet, personal hygiene and the role and responsibilities of the husband are a handful of the private issues that have somehow crept into the public domain in recent weeks.

My wife has been told that she is too skinny and that she isn't eating enough, drinking enough, sleeping enough, resting enough or even washing enough. She has been instructed what to eat, what not to eat and when not to eat it. My wife has even been sent on a guilt trip for being a vegetarian, with meat champions throwing up that tired, hackneyed old chestnut about the baby lacking the protein that comes from a good old-fashioned juicy, barbie-grilled, fat-soaked steak. These inane comments are irritating in their predictability, but what are we going to do? My wife's pregnant. All bets appear to be off.

Although our friend was only half-joking when he made reference to my domestic workload, I have been informed by others, in all seriousness, that I should be doing more around the house. I've got to take up the slack and contribute more to our relationship in the coming months. It's not only pregnant women; prospective fathers are fair game, too. My wife must do less. I must do more. This blindingly obvious gem has been handed down to me not only by close family and friends, but by perfect strangers. Of course, I just nod and thank them for their profound advice when I really want to shout, "Sod off, mate. You don't know anything about me or our relationship."

The most priceless piece of advice came from an older woman who, again, intimated that I should pull my weight more around the house and make more of an effort to spoil and pamper my pregnant wife. The advice itself was largely benign, but it was offered by a woman who had been divorced several times and had no children. I found that most incongruous. I failed my driving test several times in the 1990s but was never compelled to call Michael Schumacher and pass on a few tips for an upcoming Grand Prix.

Saturday, 2 February

As expected, there was a lot of swearing today. It was a beautiful day, but one pockmarked with expletives. We collected the baby's cot and changing table today, kindly paid for by my mother, and then we picked up the three-in-one buggy and the breastfeeding rocking chair, kindly paid for by my in-laws. When we were wandering around baby shops a fortnight ago, my father-in-law said I would have no trouble assembling all the nursery furniture. Then he wandered off, giggling.

In the interests of our enthusiasm and my patience and self-esteem, we decided to start at Mount Everest and work our way down to base camp. We started with the cot. Whistling while we worked, we unpacked the box, laid out the four sides of the cot, counted out all the screws, nuts and washers, and then read the instructions. Thirty minutes later, we were still reading the instructions. Who writes these bloody things? I'm no stranger to instructions written by English as a Foreign Language students and diagrams penned by a hippy on acid. Most of my living room came from Ikea, for heaven's sake. This was something else—a test to see how far prospective parents are willing to go. I could almost hear Sean Connery laying down the challenge. You want to be parents? What are you prepared to do? Prepare its sleeping quarters? Then what are you prepared to do? Your wife will build the changing table. You will build the cot. She will assemble the buggy. You will assemble the rocking chair. That's the parental way. That's how you get the job done.

I took this examination seriously. I knew this was only the beginning. I was literally laying the foundation. After the initial nursery assembling, it would be car-shaped beds, pirate-ship beds, beds with a built-in desk, desks with a built-in bed, TV units, DVD racks and photo collages of the prepubescent, sexless lead actors from the latest Disney musical. The cot was the first step. Fail here and I've got no chance when our teenage offspring wants its hoverboard repaired.

It wasn't as though we could phone a friend. The best handyman I know is my father-in-law, but he was of no use to us now. Fortunately, his astute, practical daughter is a chip off the old block, a shining beacon of common sense in my muddled darkness.

"We need to get these three sides together first, right," she said authoritatively. "You're holding the dropside. We don't need the dropside yet."

"Right, that makes sense," I replied. "One quick question though. What the hell's a dropside?"

Oh, I know now. I bloody know now. Fathers never forget their first dropside. The dropside does what it says on the box. It's the side of the cot that drops down to allow the parent to pick up the baby and then, with a little shimmy and a shake, pull it up and click it back into place. What could be easier? Just about everything as it turned out.

After much deliberating and some pounding of the box with a hammer, we finally got the other three sides joined together. We then tilted the cot onto its side so the one remaining empty side—the dropside—was facing up towards us. All we had to do now was ease in the dropside.

"It says the dropside must go in at a slanted angle, with one side higher than the other," my wife read from the instructions. "We'll lower my side and slide that into the groove first. Then come around and squeeze your side into the groove over there."

"Right, then … Let's do that."

I lifted my end above the cot, my wife dropped hers and we eased her side of the dropside into the groove, with surprisingly little fuss.

"That wasn't too bad," I remarked. "Come round here and let's squeeze this side in together ... Ready? Right, squeeze it into the groove."

"No, that's not working. We need to pull back the other side of the cot."

"Right, pull that side and then push in the dropside. Ready? Right, pull and push."

"No harder than that. You push and I'll pull."

"I am pushing."

"No, you're not. Nothing is happening. Push harder."

"I am!"

"Well, it's not enough. Push down harder still. It's not going in at all here."

"Ah, for fuck's sake."

God knows what the neighbours thought.

In the end, we backtracked and here's an invaluable tip for all parents preparing a nursery. You must put the other three sides of the cot together first, leaving the dropside to last, obviously, but do not tighten all the screws. After an exhaustive and futile struggle to squeeze the dropside into a gap that simply was not there, we loosened the screws on that side, widened the space, eased the dropside into the wider groove and then tightened all the screws again. Had we not tightened all the screws in the first place, we would have finished an hour earlier, but that's why swearing was invented.

Learning quickly from our mistakes, the changing table and the rocking chair were both up and rocking within twenty minutes. We paused to reflect on our collective work ethic and competent craftsmanship, and then we played. Two adults in their thirties had a most enjoyable game of mums and dads. The role-playing and miming on display were some of the finest outside of a kindergarten. Using a teddy bear, we lifted our "baby" out of the cot, pretended to change its nappy and then mother and "baby" relaxed together on the rocking chair for a breastfeeding session. She only mimed the breastfeeding; she didn't pop a boob out or anything. We're a bit daft, but we're not a danger to the public.

Sunday, 3 February

We lied to my wife's parents today. Don't blame us. Blame old wives' tales. Our parents adhere closely to the rules of folklore and superstition. Don't walk under a ladder while you are pregnant otherwise your baby will grow up to be a window cleaner. That sort of thing. My mother-in-law's pet superstition is that the furniture for a baby's nursery should not be assembled until the baby is born. It's bad luck. However, my wife and I are not superstitious and Saturday was the only free day we had to whack boxes with hammers and swear at each other. So the stuff went up. We were desperate to tell our parents that everything was successfully standing in the nursery but my mother-in-law was immovable on the issue.

"You can't get everything ready before the baby's born," she insisted while we wandered around the baby shops a few weeks ago. "It's bad luck. You can't have a baby's pram in the house with no baby in the house. It's bad luck. You're tempting fate."

This is the woman who believes that it would do the baby "the world of good" if her pregnant daughter drank a pint of Guinness every night, but leaving a pram to gather dust in the corner of the nursery will do irreparable damage.

Nevertheless, my wife had to tread carefully during her weekly online chat with her parents. These old wives' tales are really important to old wives.

"So, er, we were thinking of making a start on the nursery while we've got the chance," my wife muttered. "We've got to do it soon because we're not together that often. And I can't help Neil nearer the due date when I'm much heavier. I should be taking it easier by then."

That was a really smart move. My in-laws love an old wives' tale, but not if it potentially compromises the health of their beloved daughter.

"You've already done it, haven't you?"

"Well, you see, mum. What happened was ..."

"Look, I'm not really bothered about the furniture in the nursery. That's OK. It's just the pram. You cannot have the pram in the house until the baby's born."

"Oh, that's all right then because we've put up the cot, the changing table and the rocking chair and the pram really is in the garage."

"I knew it. You lying little bastards."

The pram really will stay in the garage. We've got nowhere to put it in the house.

My mother is also partial to an old wives' tale, but hers tend to take on a terrifying quality.

"Make sure that neither one of you runs around while you're pregnant," she has told me several times. "You don't want to fall over. Don't make your wife jump, don't scare her or jump out on her, just in case you make her fall over."

"OK, mum. I won't make her fall over."

I already know what's coming.

"It happened to me, you know, when I was carrying you," she'll say slowly. "I was ready to drop when I saw it on the stairs going home. Do you remember me telling you?"

"Yes, mum. It was a mouse."

"It was a fucking rat. And you know how I hate rats."

"I do, mum."

"It ran across my feet. I screamed and over I went, arse over tit. I fell right over. And my mum said I'd be punished for falling over while I was pregnant."

"I know she did mum, but it's not like ..."

"And look what happened? What's the biggest fear you have today? What's the only phobia you've got?"

"Suriphobia. Rodents. But I inherited that fear from you ..."

"Exactly. And my mother said I'd have a baby that looked like a rat."

"Yeah, I know that, mum, but you can't ..."

"And let's be honest, Neil, you did get those ears."

I have explained, on many occasions, that my protruding ears are a result of genes rather than the sudden intervention of Mickey Mouse. Both my father and my grandfather share a similar physical characteristic. We have larger than average ears. But my obdurate mother will not be swayed. It's all down to Stuart Little on the staircase. To underscore her beliefs, my mother has insisted that we avoid all types of rodent during the pregnancy. Collectively, we will break the vermin spell over this family.

Monday, 4 February

23 weeks today. This date marks a mini-medical milestone. At this stage, there is a chance, albeit an extremely slim one, that the baby might survive outside of the womb with extensive medical care and support. The baby's survival chances are no greater than 20 per cent, but that's not the point. The baby has the apparatus required to potentially live now. Teeth buds are sneaking up

beneath the gum line, the pancreas is developing and the baby's muscles are all moving regularly now. Every day from here on in, the baby takes another tiny step towards independence.

Wednesday, 6 February

Even David's joined the old wives' club now. He's not old, he's not a woman and he's not even British, but my old Chinese-Singaporean mate has joined our mothers' exclusive club. Although on reflection, this development is probably not as unexpected as it seems. David is a born worrier. He could worry for Singapore. We met at university in Manchester. He invited me to visit his family in Singapore for a holiday and I stayed for ten years. Since I've known him, David has worried. He worried about his university degree, his first job in Singapore, his second and third and he even found time to worry about my university degree, my first job, my apartment, my marriage, my move to Australia and, now, my first baby. He has a vested interest. My first baby will be his first Caucasian godchild so it's double jeopardy for the born worrier.

We called him to wish his family a happy Lunar New Year. This year, the year that my firstborn will come into the world, will be the Year of the Rat. I'm not even going to tell my mother. The shock could kill her. David thanked us and then agonised on our behalf.

"How is the new car?" he stressed. "Is it big enough for a baby?"

"How big do you think our baby will be, Dave?"

"Have you got a car seat yet and a buggy? Have you measured the boot?"

"Stop fretting. Everything's fine."

Undeterred, he changed tack. He didn't sound like an old

mate, but an old maid.

"What shape is the belly now?" he asked.

This was unexpected.

"Well, it's getting bigger. That's about as detailed as I can be, Dave."

"If you tell me the shape, I can tell you the sex," replied Dave, clearly getting excited. "According to Chinese tradition, if the shape is more rounded and pushing downwards, towards the ground, it is a girl, for sure. But if it's a smaller, firmer shape that sticks out in the middle, then it's a boy. So what shape is it?"

"I'm not sure. I'll call her in," I replied, quite intrigued now. "Here, mate, can you come in here for a minute. Without seeing you, Dave's going to tell us from another continent what the sex of the baby is."

I heard the toilet flush in my wife's second home before she waddled in, hands permanently stuck to the back of her hips.

"What are you going on about?" she enquired. "I can't stay long. I'm expecting to pee again any minute."

I examined my wife's stomach intently, relaying the information down the phone line at the same time.

"Well, Dave, I'd say it sticks out more in the middle. It doesn't really push towards the ground ... You think so? Right, I'll tell her ... Dave says we're going to have a boy. Yep, he's certain. He says we are definitely going to have a boy."

"Does he? That's nice of him. Thank him while I go and pee again."

Thursday, 7 February

Everyone has a theory. My sister has three boys so the laws of probability suggest we will have a girl according to my family.

Last week, my wife had a vivid dream in which she delivered a boy. She told me about the dream, then berated me for not having any dreams that may determine the sex of our unborn child. My wife and I have been discussing the subject with increasing frequency.

To borrow the most overused cliché of pregnancy, we have no preference. Honestly. And here's another one that might have you retching. We're only interested in the health of the baby. Sorry I couldn't do any better, but it's the truth. I would love to stir things up by going all misogynistic and behave like a throwback to the 1970s, insisting that I want a chip-off-the-old-block son who loves his footy and stands his old man a pint on Friday night while my wife craves a daughter so she can tie her four hairs into pigtails at family weddings, but we couldn't care less. If it's a boy, great. We'll go for a girl next time and vice versa. If nothing else, I'll enjoy the practice.

Besides, it's all gone a bit Aldous Huxley for me anyway, with parents knowing the sex of their child fifteen minutes after the egg is fertilised. They've got the wardrobe, bedroom and secondary school enrolment organised before the third trimester. We're content to play the waiting game. Hopefully, the baby's in no hurry and nor are we. If the waiting game was good enough for our mothers' generation, then it's good enough for us. That's our concession to their tradition.

So, naturally, we almost found out today by accident.

We had a mad midwife for our monthly check-up. Not mad in the straitjacket sense, but mad in the kooky, joshing doesn't-think-before-she-speaks sense. She was extremely forward, showing an utter disregard for decorum or common sense. We both liked her instantly. She invited us to take a seat while she perused the results of our belated twenty-week ultrasound scan.

"Well, it all looks good. Everything's growing in the right place and at the right place so that's good," she beamed. "Ooh, look at this. It says the baby has long bones."

She eyed my lanky frame suspiciously, tapped my wife on the knee and said, "At least, we know he's definitely the father then. Ha!"

The midwife roared with laughter while my wife blushed and I wondered whether I should kill this woman or ask her to move in with us. Still giggling, the woman with the subtle touch guided us into an adjacent room for a scan.

"Ooh, yes, the baby has got long bones, hasn't it," the midwife said, as she glided across the jelly. "You're going to have fun squeezing that one out, aren't you? Why did you marry a tall one like him, eh?"

She was going for levity. I felt like going for her larynx.

"Yes, everything looks great to me," the midwife said authoritatively. I was beginning to think she'd taken something before calling us in.

"And you know the sex of the baby, right? Because if you look here you can see …"

"No, no, no, no!"

My wife practically jumped off the bed.

"No, we don't know the sex of the baby," she said quickly. "We don't want to know."

"Don't you? Well, you'd better look away now then."

And that is the one detail that's driving me nuts. I don't know the sex of my unborn child. I don't want to know. But a midwife knows. We've had a professional relationship with this woman for twenty minutes and she now knows if we will be holding aloft a boy or a girl five months from now but we don't. It's privileged information I selfishly wish she didn't have.

Monday, 11 February

24 weeks today. Our baby should be the size of a small doll. Like most dolls, it doesn't have any genitalia that we know of because of the gender thing. On this particular issue, we appear to be part of an ever decreasing minority. My wife handed me a magazine article on the pros and cons of knowing the sex of an unborn baby. According to anecdotal evidence, or the anecdotal evidence of Australian obstetricians at least, around two-thirds of parents of second and third babies prefer to know the sex early on. That's understandable, I suppose. Romanticism has given way to practicality. There's less space in the house, possibly less money this time around, so the clothes and decorating cannot be left to chance. Idealism is a wonderful luxury, but big brother being forced to share a bedroom with little sister isn't, so needs must.

The same article suggested that around half of today's parents are eager to know the sex of their first child. I can certainly empathise with the logic. Preparing for our first baby is already keeping me awake at night, worrying about the nursery, the state of the house, the additional strain on finances and the absence of the extended family. Knowing the sex of the baby early on undoubtedly removes one major hurdle, enabling parents to hit the right side of the aisle in the baby clothes section and settle on the right shade of sky blue or Barbie pink. It's sensible. It's practical. It's wise.

It is also really boring. Where's the sense of adventure? This is a magical mystery tour and I don't want to know the destination before I get there. I'm now two-thirds of the way through this book and I've got no idea how it's going to end. I love that. Much of our excitement these days derives from comments like "It's a boy because I've got a craving for Maltesers and girls don't have balls, do they?" or "It's a girl because there was a fluttering during an episode of the *Gilmore Girls*." It's an integral part of the journey for us, and certainly one of the most enjoyable. It just seems such an anticlimax to have a doctor say "It's a boy/girl" as soon as it's possible to find out. And at the risk of veering into the spiritual, even the great Dr Derek is not big enough to be granted such a power. He lacks the amplitude to point out the gender of our unborn child. Only Nature can do that.

Besides, there is a whiff of social trends at work here. We are the "now" generation. We can't wait for anything. We can't wait for junk food, café lattes, computer downloads or even TV commercials. The index finger is permanently hovering over the fast forward button. If we can't sit through commercials and wait for the second half of a TV progamme, why should we wait nine months for our baby's sex to be revealed? Instant gratification is not only craved, but expected. Instant replay, instant coffee, instant gender. We need to get things now, doc. We need to shop now, doc. So, what's it to be, doc? Blue or pink? Barbie or Action Man? Because it's really, really important, you know.

But is it? This was the subject of tonight's debate, held in the baby clothes aisle at Kmart. We needed whites, according to my wife, lots of whites. White is the new black for sexless babies. We're going to have a bouncing baby ghost. Pinkish pictures of dollies were out of the question, along with boyish motifs of boats bobbing up and down on a pellucid sea with a sky blue background. I know most of these specials, at $4 and $5, were thrown together by some poor sod in a Chinese factory dreaming of earning a minimum wage, but baby clothes display a startling lack of originality. Girls play with dollies while boys aspire to be sailors. One particular boy's T-shirt displayed all the symbols of popular Australian sports: a cricket bat, a footy boot and a golf club. Where I grew up, that was a list of weapons.

There was very little choice. What's more, there was a clear, stereotypical division of the sexes in the aisle. The pink frilly numbers were on the left and the "hello, handsome sailor" blue shorts were on the right. There were dozens of pink dresses and blue T-shirt and shorts sets to choose from, but very little in the way of gender-neutral colours. We found a few creams and off-whites, but they looked more like factory offcuts than reasonable attire for a newborn. The reason for this is, of course, that half of the baby clothes-buying public already knows the sex of their child and can top up on the sailing boats or the frizzy-haired dolly tops.

Returning to my original question, does the colour really matter? Blue for boys and pink for girls. It's all very clichéd. *Pleasantville* à la 1950s. Despite living in enlightened times, that quiet unsaid fear continues to permeate through. Keep the boys in blue or they may end up coming home with a "special friend". Make sure that we have a Barbie girl in a Barbie world or she's bound to end up with a penchant for crew cuts, boiler suits and militant protests. If it is a boy, my baby's masculinity will not be bolstered because we dressed him up like Popeye in his formative years. I vividly recall wearing a lurid pink shirt on one of our first dates but my future wife didn't suddenly assume she was going to the bowling alley with Elton John, just a gangly teenager with ghastly dress sense.

My clothing choices had only one overriding concern.

"What about this one? This one looks great," I called out to my wife. "This little set would be ideal for the first three months. It's got dinosaurs on it. Every kid loves dinosaurs."

"It's a bit blue, isn't it?"

"Yeah, but it's only $2."

"Are all of our baby's clothes going to come from the clearance section?"

My wife pushed me away. I was contemplating buying a Father Christmas suit for a three-year-old on the grounds that it would keep our baby warm and was spectacularly reduced. She ordered me away from the clearance section once she'd noticed that I'd thrown a pair of blue pyjamas and a girl's red two-piece summer set into the trolley because they were half price.

I believe we should reject gender-neutral clothes and chop down persisting gender stereotypes. I am also a skinflint.

Wednesday, 13 February

The first stranger broke through that psychological barrier today. My wife's belly has finally reached a size where people are willing to take a gamble and risk offence. It was a brave courier making a delivery to her kindergarten who declared publicly that he could distinguish between pregnancy and obesity.

"How long have you got to go?" he asked, demonstrating an assured confidence. He did not ask "if", he went straight to "when". My wife was thrilled.

"You knew I was pregnant then? I could have just been a bit overweight," she flirted, clearly enamoured with the middle-aged man piling up toilet rolls in her classroom.

"Nah, your shape's all wrong. You can only be pregnant. I'm a grandfather. I've seen it all before. How long to go?"

"Just over four months."

The courier approved.

"Yeah, I was going to say you were about four or five months gone."

"You're the first person to come straight up and tell me that

I'm pregnant," said my gushing wife.

"Really? It's very obvious to me, love."

My wife floated home from work. The hands on the hips and the pushed-out stomach were so pronounced in the living room that she could have only topped the performance with the chorus of "Jumping Jack Flash".

Like a rolling stone, our baby is gathering momentum.

Saturday, 16 February

Observing pregnant women meet and interact is better than watching David Attenborough on TV. Like a couple of canines, they encircle each other mentally, comparing bumps, figures, complexions and maternity wear choices, before calculating due dates. They may even give the male species a quick examination to determine which couple will produce the more attractive offspring. And this all happens within moments of the initial greeting. It's a wonder they don't sniff each other's crotches.

For the first time, in my presence at least, my wife encountered another pregnant woman today. Being particularly obtuse, it took me fifteen minutes before I realised that another foetus was in the room. Feeling a pang of paternal protectiveness, I had dragged my wife down to the bank to discuss life insurance polices.

"My wife's pregnant, as you can see," I told the financial planner proudly, still oblivious to the fact that she had an equally prominent bump beneath the counter. "So we thought we'd better discuss some life insurance stuff."

"Well, that makes sense," replied the cheery young woman. "You want to be prepared for your child in case ..."

"In case I die."

The young woman blushed and then carefully and

systematically discussed the various policies on offer in that wonderfully rehearsed, bank-trained fashion that makes you feel as though you're the first person to have ever heard the spiel.

"There's one particular account you can open, called a baby boomer, where you kick off with a lump sum and leave it until the baby's eighteen. But there's no rush for that. How many months are you now?"

"Five, almost six," my wife replied. "How many months are you?"

"Oh, I'm four months."

How did my wife know that? I stood up to examine the financial planner's stomach beneath the counter.

"You're pregnant, too," I exclaimed, with far too much boyish enthusiasm. "We haven't met another one yet."

And strangely enough, we hadn't. Our current home, Geelong, is experiencing a well-documented baby boom and yet the only pregnant mammal we had come across together was a koala at the Jirrahlinga Koala and Wildlife Sanctuary. We really should mix with humans more.

I had noticed the two women eyeing each other quizzically when we first sat down and now the non-verbal inspections made sense. They were taking notes. Then the pair did a bizarre thing. They discussed all of the verboten subjects that are never touched upon between two women ordinarily, certainly not in the presence of a man. Most women would rather run down the high street in their underwear singing Tina Turner's "Private Dancer" than compare waistlines with an unfamiliar woman. The moment they become pregnant, however, they are practically holding the measuring tape for each other. Weight, diet, big bumps, protruding belly buttons, inflated boobs—nothing was off-limits between my wife and her new pregnant confidante.

The chance encounter was a lucky break for both women. For the first time, they could tick off a reassuring checklist. Dr Derek may well be a top obstetrician, but he's never peed six times a night because his uterus is shoved up against his bladder. The gentle interrogations were fascinating, watching two women work their way through their shared symptoms. Acute nausea in the third and fourth months? Check. A sudden loss of weight in the first trimester? Check (although not as much as you, you lucky cow).

Naturally, my naïve, childlike inquisitiveness inadvertently brought their checklist game to a crashing halt. The two women were comparing their steady weight gain in the second trimester when the financial planner complimented my wife.

"You've been really lucky, haven't you? You haven't put on a pound anywhere except around your belly, have you? ... I bloody have," she said, looking down at her stomach.

"Have you really?" I interjected excitedly. "What sort of diet are you on then?"

Had a pin dropped in, say, Tasmania, it would have been deafening.

The financial planner looked away. My wife looked ready to jab the nearest sharp object into my eye.

"No, what I meant was that my wife is a vegetarian and we're always keen to get enough iron and protein," I rambled. "And, you see, the thing is she lost quite a bit of weight at first, as you said, and we're eager to put it back on, aren't we mate? And, what I meant was ..."

"Yes, well, I've fixed your appointment for a week on Thursday."

My babbling really did come out wrong. The woman had a lovely, blooming figure and we are always on the lookout for practical, healthy diet tips. After much bluff and bluster on my part, I think the financial planner understood where I was coming from in the end. However, I am no longer allowed to speak to other pregnant women.

Monday, 18 February

25 weeks today. The cocoa butter moisturising stick was called out of brief retirement this evening. I hadn't seen the old friend for a while as the intense itching had subsided a couple of weeks ago. But I was handed the stick and tasked with gliding it across only the parts of my wife's body that are covered with skin. The job took a while. She insisted that the cocoa butter was summoned only to reduce the scratching, but we both knew that there was an ulterior motive. We had read that if a pregnant woman was going to be blessed with stretch marks, they usually put in an appearance from around Week 25. Moisturisers will do little to stop them spreading. Even the divine cocoa butter stick is rendered impotent against the invading might of stretch marks. These lines are determined by genetics rather than The Body Shop. Nevertheless, the frequent use of moisturisers may help a little in tackling, or at least minimising, any marks on the breasts.

That brings me to my other new job. I was informed this evening that I will be asked, at regular intervals, to examine my wife's swollen belly, boobs and bum. There was a time—it now feels like 1974—when I had tentatively ventured into such territories with boyish enthusiasm to locate erogenous zones. An older, wiser man, I must now track down the emergence of stretch marks. My suggestion to take a trowel and a tube of gap filler with me was swiftly rejected.

I tried to point out that those silvery white marks, should

they eventually appear, will serve as a permanent souvenir of our first baby.

"Can't I just have a teddy bear or something?" my wife asked.

Tuesday, 19 February

The evening was spent perusing collections of nursing bras. These ingenious contraptions contain zips, fasteners or pouches that can be whipped open in a breastfeeding emergency. Think Janet Jackson's wardrobe malfunction, but with a starving baby at the other end rather than Justin Timberlake. Nursing bras tend to be big, coming in three sizes: large, extra large and parachute. Sensibly, my wife thought it practical to buy larger, supportive, nursing bras now and kill two birds with one stone.

Her concern is understandable. My wife's breasts could stop traffic. I am beginning to think nursing bras were given their name because their occupants look like Hattie Jacques, the old matron from the *Carry On* movies (a lovely cultural reference for my nan's generation). Some of the ones that my wife picked up belonged only on a beach in the Bahamas, stretched between two palm trees.

"Well, what about this one?" my wife asked, waving what looked like a white tablecloth at me.

"You really think you're going to need one that big?"

"I will in a couple of weeks. And I can use it when I'm breastfeeding."

"You could use it as a beach towel."

I was asked to critique colour, fabric, size and efficiency (how fast one could whip out a boob to feed the little one). As the fashion show progressed, my wife made me stand outside the changing rooms holding various bras while she went inside and tried on a couple at a time. I was handed two tent-sized beauties—one white, one peach—informed that they were too big and ordered to return them to the rack. Naturally, at that moment, a middle-aged guy wearing grubby overalls wandered past. He smiled at me.

"I'd go for the white one if I were you," he said.

Friday, 22 February

I was called Mrs Mum today. The timing was cosmic. On the day that my mother celebrated her birthday on the other side of the planet, someone called me Mrs Mum. I took the gentle jibe as a compliment although I'm not entirely sure it was meant that way.

A friend asked what my plans were after the birth.

"Ooh, you won't see me for dust, mate," I said. "I won't be going anywhere. It'll be baby time."

"Ha, Mrs Mum," he replied. "You're going to play Mrs Mum then?"

I'm not sure about that, but I'll have a stab at playing Mr Dad.

My wife and I have been discussing our postnatal work arrangements a lot lately. With the third trimester looming, I'm sure most to-be parents do the same around now. I cannot lie. We are in a rather fortuitous position. In theory, for at least the first six months or so, we could both be stay-at-home parents, whatever that is supposed to mean. My wife is a teacher, which means she can return to the same job after unpaid maternity leave of up to eighteen months. I am a writer, which means I can work in my boxer shorts in my office beside the nursery during naps and breastfeeding sessions and try to convince myself that it constitutes real work. I have deliberately navigated my career, taking several pay cuts along the way, to try and reach this position before any children came along.

It has not been a career by accident. My parents divorced when I was four. Inevitably, I was always going to be paranoid about how much time I spend with my children. My background, drenched as it is in working-class stereotypes, takes care of that. Greater London council estate, broken home, working mother, latch-key kid, my little sister's babysitter after school, once-a-week dad, child maintenance and two part-time jobs by the age of twelve, I was a sociologist's definitive cliché (I must pause for a moment to inject a litre of heroin and rob my local 7-Eleven). My upbringing was as much a part of the 1980s as Rubik's cubes, shoulder pads and *The Karate Kid*. My mother played Mrs Mum and Mr Dad. She was the man of the house, the sole breadwinner and a once-only cheerleader. I allowed her to watch one of my junior football matches. After the game, I ordered her never to return. I can still see her now, standing on the touchline with all of the other dads, shouting the wrong sports clichés at the wrong times.

"Go on, Neil, you show 'em, mate," she cried from the halfway line. "Don't be afraid to tackle. Get stuck in, boy."

I was the goalkeeper.

We represented Barking Juniors. My mum was barking. Out of desperation, I gave her a few basic pointers on cheers, heckles and general phrases of encouragement for a goalkeeper at half-time. She was allowed to stay for the second half on the promise that she only shouted the correct football cliché.

This she did. All the bloody time.

"Safe hands, Neil. Safe hands," she shouted constantly throughout the match. "He's got safe hands, my boy. Safe hands. Look at him! Safe hands, boy."

"I haven't got the ball, mum," I hissed. "It's at the other end of the pitch."

"It doesn't matter. You've got safe hands, Neil. Safe hands!"

At the time, I found those incidents excruciating. Teenage boys are loath to admit that they even have a mother, let alone one who heckles them in front of their teammates. Later, of course, I thought the story was amusing and my mother still occasionally shouts "safe hands" if I ever drop something in the kitchen. Today, I think there is a slight sadness to it all. The memory of my mother standing alone among 25 working-class blokes is now dipped in so much pathos that the scene belongs in a Mike Leigh film. I feel sorry for the woman who was clearly out of her depth and used my little sister as moral support, a shield to hide her exposure in no-woman's land. I also have considerable empathy for the younger me who was doubly determined to impress his mother because she was playing both parents in a man's world.

This isn't a tears of a clown routine. Any lingering resentment of what I may have missed out on in childhood has given way to the realisation that my one-parent model nurtured me with the values of independence, resilience, a social conscience and a disturbing infatuation with indomitable women. I'm too self-aware to give all that up, even for a memory bank filled with two-parent family anecdotes.

That leads, of course, to the oft-repeated parental paradox. We want our children to develop into responsible, selfless, autonomous individuals but are reluctant to recreate the more austere environment to make that more likely. We front every sentence with "In my day, we had to ...", but we don't want our children to have to do the same. We cherish our self-reliant childhood but will fight tooth and nail to avoid repeating it with our own children. We want selflessness without the sacrifice, resilience without the struggle and adult independence without the childhood independence. I hope my children share many of the values that were shaped by my thrifty childhood, but I'm not going to divorce my wife, see my child only once a week and provide nothing but the basic necessities to make that happen. I want Darwinism. I also want to buy my child a fancy ice cream whenever it asks for one.

I'll take my chances by being a much more stay-at-home dad. Still, our child will be forced to take a part-time job in a Western Australian copper mine during the school holidays. That should keep its Nike-covered feet on the ground.

Our child will need all the grounding it can get because, according to a recent survey, my mere presence around the house is sure to mess things up anyway.

Searching the subject of stay-home dads online, I came across the emotive headline "Why a stay-home dad can be bad for boys (but not girls)". In a 2007 article in Britain's *Daily Mail*, it was reported that dads who bring up their infant sons could damage their sons' future chances in life. This was the finding of The Bristol Project, which was financed by the British Government's Economic and Social Research Council to document the lives of children living with both their natural parents.

After investigating 6,000 British families, researchers suggested that boy toddlers looked after by stay-at-home dads can be slower and less ready for education than other children when they start school. Strangely, this phenomenon does not apply to girls. The reasons offered why mums might be better at looking after children than dads were biological and cultural. Breastfeeding is one particular, and obvious, advantage. Although I'm not quite sure how this is going to bolster Little Johnny's sorting and sequencing skills in kindergarten. The survey added that women could be biologically more confident and skilled in raising children and I would not disagree with that. However, many fathers might take issue with the claim that there might be "harmful emotional effects" due to the mother's absence.

Rather than scare stay-at-home fathers back to the office, the article's conservative intention appeared to be to terrify working mothers into running and screaming all the way home and into the arms of their disadvantaged toddlers. By the time these wicked mothers return, Little Johnny will be sitting on the sofa watching football, eating peanuts with one hand and scratching his testicles with the other. I've already promised my wife that this will only happen on Saturday nights.

I do not wish to denigrate the 2007 findings of Bristol University but I will point out the blindingly obvious. Whether they stay at home, go to work or work at home, there are fabulous fathers and shit mothers. There are also shit fathers and magnificent mothers. There are even shit mothers and shit fathers who produce—all together now—a little shit.

That's why I'm more than willing to take a gamble and risk the wrath of conservatives everywhere. I would love to have a crack at working from home if I have the opportunity. Whether that makes me a Mrs Mum or a stay-at-home dad, I don't know (or care). I'll leave the terminology to the experts. I'll just try to be a father.

At least my old mum is confident. She is positive the baby will be in safe hands.

Monday, 25 February

26 weeks today. We've made it to the end of the second trimester. Everything appears to be on course. My wife continues to urinate

every three hours throughout the night and we are working our way through more green shoots and leaves than a panda to sustain protein levels.

The baby will now weigh around 750 g (or around 1.7 pounds in old money), which is still no more than 25 per cent of its expected birth weight, if the baby goes to full term. My wife was delighted to learn that three-quarters of the baby's weight will now be piled on in the final fourteen weeks. She sighed and muttered something about preparing a spinach and ricotta lasagne to deal with the energy surge required.

Curiously, babies can cry by the end of the second trimester. Considering they spend all their time in the safest, most sterile environment any human being will ever encounter, I'm not sure what they've got to cry about. In a perverse sense, Nature has afforded the baby almost four months to develop its crying skills so by the time feeding/crapping/sleeping time comes along, the art of stripping the skin from our faces with one lung-busting scream will be perfected.

Tuesday, 26 February

For over a month now, my wife has grown exasperated at my inability to share in the baby's flutterings. She is desperate for me to feel our baby's presence, but equally aware that the initial movements of pregnancy are not a shared experience. She has been waiting patiently for the fluttering to give way to kicking; for internal sensations to be felt externally so that daddy can join the fold. My wonderful wife is eager for me to make a physical connection, too.

Tonight, it happened.

In one electrifying, but terrifying, moment, we made a

collective breakthrough. The incident was brief and timeless; surreal and sublime; frightening and euphoric; natural and unnatural. For the first time, father and child were formally introduced—our baby kicked me in the bloody head.

My wife had called me into the bedroom, dragging my head towards her stomach on an entirely different pretext.

"Come and have a listen," she said, pressing my head against the bump. "I read that by the end of the second trimester you can hear the baby's heartbeat if you stick your ear against my uterus."

"I can't even find my own heartbeat so how do you expect me to find this one?"

"Just shut up and have a go ..."

"All right, all right ... Now, where am I supposed to ... Argh! What the hell was that?"

I jumped off the bed backwards and inadvertently threw myself up against the wardrobe. The very millisecond I infringed upon the baby's territory, the bugger booted me in the head. Our short, spiritual connection was truly beautiful and I behaved appropriately.

I shit myself.

"Did you see that?" I screamed from across the bedroom at my nonplussed wife.

"What happened? What happened?"

"The baby kicked me in the head. I can't believe it. The baby kicked me in the head."

My wife sat up slowly, clearly delighted.

"That's brilliant. What did it feel like?"

"Weird. Bloody weird. Like in *Alien*."

"What?"

"You know, *Alien*. That scene when it pops out of John Hurt's stomach and ..."

"Calm down and come back over here."

My reassuring wife guided me back to the edge of the bed, but I was too confused to sit down. The moment was exhilarating, but also a trifle scary. A fragile being had lashed out when I had invaded its space and I was unwilling to take what I perceived to be a risk again. And, yes, being kicked in the side of the face unexpectedly by my unborn child freaked me out on more levels than I could possibly comprehend.

"Do you want to try again?" my excited wife asked.

"No way."

"Go on, I can feel the baby's quite restless now. Have another go."

With more than a little reluctance, I pressed my head slowly against my wife's bump. Then I pulled back suddenly. I tried again and again, but I always hesitated and recoiled. My confused manner can only be compared to a recent encounter with a baby crocodile at a town fête. The crocodile's owner had set up a mini-petting enclosure of native animals. When I stroked the crocodile's head, it whipped around and brushed my hand. The crocodile's jaws were taped up so I knew that the baby snapper couldn't bite me but I was still reluctant to stroke its head a second time. Now, I'm not comparing my unborn child to a man-eating reptile, but the logic was the same in the sense that there wasn't any. Like stroking the taped-up head of a crocodile, the sensation of feeling my child kick me from inside the womb was so outlandish that to try and relive the experience felt precarious despite knowing that the risks were negligible.

Fortunately, my wife sorted me out.

"It's a baby, you silly sod," she said. "Now get down there and see if you can get it to kick you in the head again."

I did as I was told, but the baby did not comply with its

mother's wishes. My increasing bravery, along with my wife pinning me down against my will, allowed me to spend another fifteen minutes with my ear jammed against her uterus. There was no further kicking, but I didn't care. As my irrational fear of my child's feet gradually subsided, elation took over. My baby had kicked me.

I had felt my baby's presence and what a kick in the head it was, too. How lucky can one guy be?

Thursday, 28 February

My wife woke up in the early hours to find my head resting on her exposed stomach.

"What are you doing? It's almost two o'clock," my groggy wife mumbled.

"I'm listening out for any kicking," I whispered enthusiastically.

"Have you heard anything?" she asked, her tiredness unable to curb her curiosity.

"Nah, not yet. I'll give it another ten minutes and see what happens."

My wife smiled and went back to sleep.

The Third Trimester

Saturday, 1 March

We were told to collect our handwritten stickers with our names on and take a seat. The wearing of a handwritten sticker can only signify one of two occasions: you are on a school trip or you are participating in a seminar.

"And you are?" the jaunty midwife-cum-lecturer asked in that optimistic first-day-of-school teacher's voice.

"Neil Humphreys," I muttered.

"Ah, yes, and you're married to Stacy?"

"No, I'm not."

"Oh, really?"

"Yeah, I think so. I was at the wedding."

The midwife referred back to her clipboard and scanned the day's list of students. Her finger found my name.

"Ah, there you are," she replied brightly. "No, you're not married to Stacy, are you? We're still waiting for Stacy. OK, take your sticker, Neil, and have a seat."

The chairs were arranged in the typical, horseshoe shape favoured at these sessions to facilitate "icebreaker" activities and "informal" discussions. A couple of laminated posters of foetuses had been Blu-tacked to the walls. These may have rammed home the point that we had not gathered for a debate on diabetes but did little to disguise the dull, musty room's regular function of serving as a medical meeting room.

As we had had some difficulty finding the venue, the horseshoe was already 75 per cent full by the time that we got there. Not surprisingly, the chairs in the middle were still vacant so we were forced to sit at the top of the class as it were. Bladder-squashed women had already nabbed all the seats by the exit.

"I'm going to have to walk across the middle of the room when I need to go," my wife whispered.

"Why didn't you go earlier?" I asked, keeping a close watch on the classroom door. I was starting to worry about the absent Stacy.

"I did go earlier," she hissed.

"Well, try and last until the tea break."

She lasted less than an hour. The midwife's cervix had only dilated by around 4 centimetres (on the whiteboard) when my wife felt the urge.

We were still waiting for Stacy and a couple of stragglers to grace us with their presence. I'm not superstitious but I wouldn't want to be late as a pregnant woman. Much to my relief, Stacy finally arrived with her partner. Like all latecomers, they made a decent stab at invisibility by dashing straight to the empty seats beside us.

"Hello there. Thanks for coming," the midwife's voice boomed across the room. "Can you come and get your name tags, please?"

The latecomers were the centre of attention.

"As you've arrived a little late, I'll need to check the register," the midwife continued, waving the register above her head. "If you don't get the stickers, I won't know who you are. Ha ha."

The uncomfortable, forced jollity merely compounded the embarrassment. Taking the seats near my wife, I heard the guy whisper, "Get the stickers."

"I'm not getting the stickers," his heavily pregnant partner retorted. "You get the bloody stickers."

This was shaping up to be a memorable day. The guy trotted over to the midwife's desk, ripped off the stickers, nodded to the midwife without making eye contact and returned to his puce partner. When the group was dismissed for lunch a few hours later, they were the first ones back in class.

Antenatal classes provide an invaluable service, particularly for first-time parents like us. In broad strokes, today's class planned to focus on the final stages of pregnancy and the labour itself, including the medical procedures and interventions, physical preparation, the stages of labour, the sources of pain and pain relief and the induction of labour (natural vs Caesarean). The seminar promised to include everything us first-timers needed to know about the birth, which was everything.

I still found it hard to take the class seriously. Perhaps *The Office* has made me cynical, but almost every adult class I have attended, with the forced bonding and transparent team-building initiatives, has had the irony-free shadow of David Brent hanging over it. When I was working for a newspaper in Singapore a few years ago, I attended a seminar that pledged to facilitate my "social skills". I vividly recall the lecturer, who was younger than me even then, rebuking me for being disruptive and insisted that I take the role-playing exercises seriously. My social skills were suitably "facilitated" though. I completed the course without telling him to piss off.

I feared the worst at the antenatal class when the midwife asked us to introduce ourselves to the class and—here's the rub—list all the hobbies and pastimes of our partners. This was an icebreaker working on so many levels. The first couple opened with the guy saying, "This is my wife. And her hobby is shopping."

The quip brought the house down. Seminar and workshop audiences are always extraordinarily polite when it comes to the paucity of comedy on offer. Lecturers have long reminded me of tennis players. Not just any tennis player but the ones referred to as "personalities", like Henri Leconte and 2008 Australian Open champion Novak Djokovic. These guys only have to wink at an audience and spectators positively wet themselves. Poke out your tongue in a pub and your audience will collectively roll their eyes. Do it at Wimbledon, however, and they're rolling in the aisles and thanking you for being a rare personality in the modern sporting world of surly superstars.

Adult classes are not much different. Lecturers and participants get some easy laughs from some woeful material. Audiences who have spent much of their Saturday watching mentally challenged mothers willingly deliver babies for a TV documentary will pretty much laugh at anything.

The midwife moved on to the next couple. When it was the husband's turn, and I swear this happened, he said, "This is my wife … And she also likes shopping."

Well, I think some of the participants are still laughing. We were going to get nothing done at this rate. Of course, I could always rely on my straight-shooting wife to tell it like it is.

"This is my husband, Neil," said Mrs Empirical. "He likes to read and write."

No one laughed. Why would they?

"He likes to read and write?" I hissed. "Was that the best you could come up with?"

"Well, you do like to read and write," she replied.

"So do six-year-olds. Why didn't you tell them I like sand and water play, too?"

We finished the icebreaker game to give our aching sides a rest and moved on to the serious business of delivering babies. The midwife produced a malleable baby doll and a plastic pelvis and proceeded to push one through the other. Talk about square peg in a round hole. The dimensions involved made the delivery appear impossible, even with a silent, docile doll. As the midwife struggled to shove the head through the plastic contraption, the women smiled knowingly. Their wide-eyed partners looked horrified.

Not surprisingly, the midwife was preoccupied with pain. There will be pain. There will be blood. The ominous promises came thick and fast.

"When the cervix dilates, the festival of pain begins but it is always pain with a purpose," she said.

The midwife was particularly fond of repeating the phrase "pain with a purpose". We returned to it frequently, but never more so than when we reached the "fuck it" stage. We listened dutifully, but somewhat intermittently, through all the contractions—from the moment the mucus plug comes away, the "show" of blood appears and the cervix begins to open right up until the cervix hits the 8-cm mark. That indicates the beginning of the "fuck it" stage. Everyone in the room paid attention during this stage.

The midwife called it the transition stage. My wife provided its new name. It's when the cervix dilates from 8 to 10 cm. During this stage, the woman experiences the most intense and most frequent contractions. Consequently, it's often at this point that the exhausted, emotionally shattered mother is ready to wave the white flag. This is the stage of labour that is portrayed in all the movies, and is when everything seems to start happening. Women often feel nauseous, some vomit and there is lots of bloody discharge. The transition stage can last a couple of minutes or it can last a couple of hours. We are not looking forward to it. This is when mothers must be motivated to make that final push.

"This is when I'll be ready to say 'fuck it'," my wife whispered.

After a coffee break, we were rewarded with that traditional classroom treat—the educational video. We settled back to watch a documentary entitled *Birthing My Way*. It should have been called *Birthing My Way in the 1980s*. Is there an educational programme or a corporate video that wasn't made in the 1980s? Was there a shortage back then? *Birthing My Way* chronicled the delivery choices of a handful of mothers. These mothers discussed which techniques worked for them, but it was hard to hear them over their pink blusher and purple eye shadow. The 1980s did no one any favours fashionwise, but it was a horrendous decade for Australians. The first mother interviewed looked like Sheena Easton in a garish, knitted jumper. She was championing the benefits of pelvic rocking, but I could only picture her belting out "For Your Eyes Only". The entire documentary had a new wave whiff about it. Even Sheena Easton's toddler was dressed in more frills than Adam and the Ants.

The problem I have with any documentary of this nature is that I find it exceedingly difficult to take seriously anyone who is happy to have a documentary crew film her performing her naked, pelvic rocking routine in the shower. As I watched the heavily pregnant Sheena rotate her roomy hips under the shower while her disturbingly thin partner spooned her from behind, I admired her willingness to suffer publicly for our greater good. Was she a selfless and willing guinea pig in an invaluable documentary? Absolutely. Would I perform naked, pelvic rocks for a film crew? I'd rather perform naked on jagged rocks.

Sheena Easton mentioned a word that I had not heard since my biology classes in secondary school and I had had no idea what it meant then—perineum. This anatomical term cropped up quite a lot. The perineum is the diamond-shaped area between the legs that incorporates the anus and, in the female's case, the vagina. During labour, a woman's perineum can tear. In rare cases, the sphincter is also ripped. Ooh, did you wince then? We certainly did when Sheena Easton, and later our midwife, detailed the complications that can lead to the perineum being ripped. If the primary goal of every woman in that room was a healthy first baby, then the unsaid secondary goal was an intact perineum. If the perineum is damaged during childbirth, the pelvic structure may be weakened, the recovery is prolonged and more painful and there can even be long-term incontinence. The midwife said some of her mothers admitted afterwards that they had never experienced pain like it. The room went awfully quiet. A ripped perineum is not an advert for natural birth.

After the video came the test. We were divided into three teams to jot down the different pain relief techniques demonstrated on the video. The three teams were given names—the Quiet, the Practical and the Hippies—by me several hours later. My wife and I were part of the Quiet team. All of the members were in their early thirties, a little reluctant to be "tested" and even less willing to engage in small talk with strangers whose only connection was a lot of sex six months ago. We were still young enough to be self-conscious, but old enough to cynically believe that the exercise was redundant. The Practical team, on the other hand, left us trailing and rightly so. Mostly older, no-nonsense first-time parents, they utilised their chance to brainstorm exercises to save their perinea (that's the plural, I looked it up). One particular woman was not only the most vocal, but the most eager to absorb every scrap of information. She put our team's self-conscious jokes and flippancy into perspective. She was in her early forties and having her first child. Pain relief was a priority.

For the Hippies, pain relief was going to come about through good karma. Their spiritual suggestions transcended Sheena Easton's video. Soft music, meditation, rhythmic breathing and a tranquil environment complimented with aroma burners were some of the ways expectant mothers could sail through delivery on a wave of positive vibes. Doctors cannot always stop a woman's perineum from ripping but a few strategically placed joss sticks might.

The youngest mother-to-be in the Hippies team was also one of the loudest, not because of her age, but because of her partner. He wasn't there. The poor girl was the only pregnant woman in the class not to be accompanied by the father. No one else in the class had an issue with this, but she clearly did. She overcompensated for her husband's absence by mentioning him at every opportunity in a loud, trying-too-hard voice.

"What is the best pain relief? I reckon it's to lock my husband in the room with me," she bellowed. "I can just see my husband doing some pelvic rocking. He'd run a mile ... My husband won't want to do that ... My husband will have to watch his own breathing."

I felt sorry for her.

The midwife rounded off the pain relief discussion by suggesting the most unorthodox method of the lot—a mirror between the legs. The theory goes that if the woman can actually see, rather than just feel, the contractions, she can prepare for them and react accordingly. She will know when to push and when to relax, when to expend energy and when to hold back. The mirror can make for a more symbiotic and cooperative relationship between mother and baby.

"I can see the logic," I whispered to my wife.

"If you think I'm going to stand over a mirror and look down at my bits, you've got another thing coming," she replied.

It was time for lunch.

The afternoon session revolved around the drugs used during labour and the C-word. Will we be too posh to push and too posh to take the pain? The midwife discussed the three drugs commonly used: nitrous oxide (laughing gas), pethidine (an opiate) and the always popular epidural (needle near the spinal cord; honey, I can't feel my legs). Nitrous oxide always brings to mind perverted dentists, at least it does for me. The only time I come across the drug is when I'm reading about a dentist who had his wicked way with a patient while she was under laughing gas. On the plus side, the drug kicks in immediately and does not accumulate (after two hours there should be no traces of nitrous oxide in the body). However, it can be a bit of a head-spinner and may cause nausea and loss of self-control.

Being the prudish, and probably naïve, couple that we are, pethidine does not really appeal. It is an opiate (or an opioid analgesic drug to be precise). It is a narcotic, a drug that deadens pain and feeling. Basically, it is a synthetic version of morphine. The midwife referenced the drug in the same sentence as heroin, which hardly sold us on the product. She claimed that it was once common to prescribe pregnant women with heroin during labour. That's all you need. Your wife and baby leaving hospital looking like Sid and Nancy. On top of this, research has suggested a potential link between the exposure of some babies to pethidine during labour and their later development of an addiction to opiate drugs as teenagers. This is by no means conclusive and I do not want to get all Tom Cruise about it. If my wife is screaming in distress, we will allow the midwife to administer whatever is necessary. But if my wife staggers out of the hospital slurring Lou Reed songs, litigation proceedings will follow.

Now, epidurals are tricky, aren't they? Surely, on balance, no mother would want to be largely numb from the waist down, missing out on many of the birthing sensations and possibly lacking the ability to even feel their child entering the world.

The epidural comes with the obvious, but slight, risks of muscle paralysis, nerve damage and, much more common, pounding headaches. That's aside from the terrifying notion of a doctor injecting drugs through a catheter into the epidural space around the spine. All things being equal, I'd rather keep my wife's spine out of it. You can tell I'm a naïve, idealistic, first-time parent.

The midwife pointed out that around 35 per cent of her patients take the needle in the back. She offered a similar percentage for Caesarean sections. Around 35 per cent of admissions at our hospital opted for the knife. When push comes to shove, not everyone wants to push. I queried the percentage and made an immediate, lifelong enemy of the oldest pregnant woman in the room.

"Sorry to interrupt but you said that over a third of the women who come here have C-sections?" I asked. "That seems like a high number. What are the reasons?"

"What do you mean?" replied the puzzled midwife.

"Well, I mean, does the figure just refer to emergency C-sections? Or does it also include couples who want to get home to watch the football?"

The question was valid, but my edgy, blustering (and entirely unsuccessful) attempt at humour was inappropriate, and unappreciated. Ten pregnant women fixed me with glares that indicated they would have happily stuck an epidural needle into my tongue.

"I am having a C-section delivery," the oldest pregnant woman said slowly, her eyes drilling two holes through my forehead. "It is an elective C-section, on the doctor's advice, because of my age."

The room fell so quiet that you could have heard a pregnant lady drop. As everyone looked at me, I contemplated performing an emergency C-section on my own cranium.

"Well, er, it's time to show the video on C-sections," the midwife chimed in. Thank God for the midwife. Thank God for cheesy, educational videos.

The video's title got the biggest laugh of the afternoon. Several women in disturbing afros provided sound bites on their C-section births before the title popped up on the screen—*I Was in Stitches.*

So were all the men in the room after that. Most of the women chuckled. My adversary, the oldest pregnant woman, was visibly disgusted. I made sure that I laughed really loudly. The narrator described the bloody deliveries with a gleeful, upbeat pleasantness that was rather macabre. As doctors stitched up a dazed, exhausted woman's gaping wound, he cheerily said, "And just 30 stitches and 20 minutes later, all was well."

It was difficult not to empathise with some of the women on the documentary. Desperate for a natural birth, they were advised to have a C-section because of medical risks beyond their control. Months later, one particular woman, who had a penchant for tight perms and luminous, knitted jumpers, was still struggling with the guilt. The delivery team had clearly made the right call and the mother emerged relatively unscathed, physically at least. But then, I'm not entirely sure she had been dealt a full deck of cards to begin with.

Dabbing her eyes with a sopping hanky, the teary-eyed woman mumbled, "I felt ashamed that I couldn't deliver my baby vaginally."

I had to cover my mouth. I know it's puerile, but I had never heard the female organ used as an adverb before. God knows, we bandied the noun about enough in secondary school and used it in every juvenile context imaginable, but never as an adverb.

I have since spent far too much time pondering its usage and have concluded that "vaginally" could only be realistically used in this context. No one turns up in a Bangkok bar and says, "We've come to watch the Thai girl play ping pong vaginally."

The knitted jumper lady was the only interviewee to utter the adverb and I can only thank her for making a profound contribution to my vocabulary and our birthing beliefs. All things being equal, we are even more hopeful that our baby will be delivered vaginally.

Sunday, 2 March

Celebrities who opt for an elective Caesarean get a hard time in the media. Just a day after watching the incomparable *I Was in Stitches*, I read that singer Christina Aguilera had gone for the C-section cut followed by a US$1.5 million photo shoot with her new baby for a glossy magazine. Well, don't we all? In the interview, the pop star claimed that she had vetoed the idea of a natural birth because she had heard horrific stories about tearing and some celebrity mothers being caught in some equally terrifying post-paparazzi shots. OK, the first bit is true. Aguilera was keen on a peaceful environment and, obviously, such a serene setting can only be accomplished in a room full of magazine photographers, a lighting crew, a make-up unit and a handful of publicists.

Victoria Beckham went for C-sections for all three of her children and was castigated in the media for being "too posh to push". Some sympathetic commentators have suggested that these celebrity C-sections (and there are a lot) could be a result of tokophobia, a fear of childbirth delaying a lucrative photo shoot. (*Tokos* comes from the Greek word meaning "childbirth".)

Interestingly, a 2008 British study found that almost half of pregnant women who request a Caesarean section do so because they have a genuine fear of childbirth. In fact, it's estimated that one in seven women may be tokophobic. It's thanks to all those damned horror stories from our dear, beloved friends and families. You know the ones. Your mother insists that her labour lasted 78 hours and that the resulting baby was so big, the doctors christened it Moby Dick and sent in a Japanese whaling fleet.

At the risk of sounding Darwinist and, well, like a man, part of the problem is that we now have a choice. Natural births have been coming along quite nicely since our lineage diverged from that of chimpanzees around five million years ago, something I constantly struggle with when I hand money over to my obstetrician's receptionist each month after being told, yet again, that "everything looks fine." Of course everything looks fine. For all our faults, our species continues to surpass itself in the biological fields of shagging and reproduction.

The reason my wife will have a choice three months from now can be attributed, I believe, to an illiterate pig gelder. History judges Jakob Nufer to be the first person to successfully perform a Caesarean section where the woman survived, in this case his extremely grateful wife. Nufer spent his days working with the anatomy of pigs. Whether he took one look at his bulging wife and picked out enough anatomical similarities to inspire confidence is not for me to say. But on one memorable day in the year 1500, the Swiss farmer took matters into his own hands. The story goes that his wife endured several, painful days in labour and the poking and prodding of thirteen midwives. I suspect only one midwife did the actual poking and prodding. The other twelve probably stood around the distressed woman for a bit of village gossip, sighing dramatically and making comments like "Ooh, this is nothing. We had one last week who gave birth after a seven-year labour. By the time the baby came out, her husband had died of a medieval, debilitating skin disease."

That was enough for Nufer. After detailing all his husbandry skills and experience, he was granted permission from the local authorities to perform a C-section. The medieval farmer's hands went where no other medieval farmer's hands had gone before and that must be saying something. He grabbed his favourite gelding knife and sliced open his beloved wife.

She survived. And so did the baby. By all accounts (well, just the one, and that wasn't written until 82 years later), the Caesarean baby lived to the age of 77. I have also read sources that claim the wife lived to the age of 77. That's either some spooky karma or conflicting historical sources. Regardless, I refuse to challenge the veracity of Nufer's story. I always want to believe a rabbit was pulled from the hat. I want to believe in magic. A medieval pig farmer from Switzerland pulled off a medical feat of incomparable magnitude so that five hundred years later, my wife will have a choice and Christina Aguilera could avoid tearing her perineum in childbirth. For that, we should all be eternally grateful.

Monday, 3 March

27 weeks today. Our baby is into its third and final trimester. The finish line is not yet in sight, but the bell for the last lap has been rung. We're heading for the maximum foetal growth phase and, more entertainingly, the baby can develop hiccups from this stage. Our wrinkled baby should now be assuming the looks it will present to us at birth. When I met my wife, my mother and late grandmother remarked that she looked like a cross between

a young Olivia Newton John and Jodie Foster. My mother always said I had a great face for radio. I hope our child inherits my wife's looks and my mother's acerbic wit.

To celebrate the third trimester, an unexpected baby's parcel arrived today from my mother. The parcel in itself was not unexpected. She has been sending parcels from England regularly—romper suits, pyjamas and blankets have been making their way from one end of the planet to the other—and we are most grateful. We appreciate her eagerness to be involved from afar, but I know my mother—nanna's marking her territory. She's strengthening the elastic bonds of family and kinship and why not?

Her generation, and particularly that of her parents, contributed to the fragmentation of traditional, deep-rooted working-class communities. My grandparents' generation experienced first-hand the great upheaval that came with slum clearance in London, being scattered to estates in places like Dagenham and Barking in neighbouring Essex. A decent council house and socio-economic mobility were gained, but a sense of the extended family was lost. Family support systems were further weakened by Thatcherism's right-to-buy housing scheme. My parents' generation withdrew behind the doors of their mortgaged kingdoms and the previously close-knit, extended family was locked outside. Then my generation came along and cut family ties completely by buggering off to the other side of the world.

Like a number of my generation's children, my baby will be lucky if it sees its grandparents once a year. That will be hard on our parents. British working-class families have long struggled with socially mobile children and our families took a while to accept our decision to live and work overseas. To compensate, my mum is sending little gifts for our baby on an almost weekly basis. They are practically stamped "property of nanna". Our child will not be able to move in its nursery without touching, seeing, smelling, eating, wearing or playing with something that was bought by its overseas grandparents. They may live in England, but our parents are already omnipresent in our Australian nursery.

My mother certainly is. Today, she surpassed herself. She sent over a West Ham United vest and flannel and a pair of West Ham baby bottles. That really was most unexpected. To my knowledge, my mother never bought me any West Ham merchandise when I was growing up. Yet here she is, striding purposefully into the traditionally alpha-male world of football superstores to kit out her unborn grandchild in claret and blue. She spent my formative years playing both mother and father and that instinctive, dual-parenting protectiveness is kicking in again now.

It is only a matter of time before my child is sitting on her knee in a pub, singing football songs and sipping its first pint.

Monday, 10 March

28 weeks today. Our baby should be the size of a football by now. That was cause for much celebration until I realised that I was reading an Australian book. The author was referring to an oval-shaped Aussie Rules ball. It was several moments before I realised that my wife would look like a Weeble if she really was carrying a soccer ball-shaped baby. Nevertheless, our child could be as long as 35 cm and has officially outgrown most standard 30-cm rulers. Speaking of things that are measured with school rulers, if our baby is a boy, his balls are dropping too, to borrow my father-in-law's vernacular. In other words, the testes begin their all-important descent from 28 weeks.

My wife's breasts may also begin to leak colostrum from now on. Colostrum, also known as immune milk or first milk, is critically important. High in protein, carbohydrates and antibodies but low in fat (which newborns struggle to digest), it is a remarkable cocktail of goodness for a newborn. The nutrients in it are concentrated and it even has a laxative effect that will make our baby's first poo more manageable. I have been tasked with monitoring my wife's breasts for colostrum leakage. I find the job most ironic. It's like looking at attractive jewellery through the shop window because the shop is closed.

Thursday, 13 March

Dr Derek was in the house. The man with the delivery plan made a fleeting appearance in his own surgery today. Dr Derek's presence was so unexpected that we felt strangely privileged and unworthy of his attention. Before he strolled authoritatively into the room, we were chugging along nicely with the midwife. There were no inappropriate remarks about the father's gangly frame, just the usual exchange of urine and a chat about my wife's diet while a CD of calming, world muzak played quietly in the background. My wife has been suffering from leg cramps at night, a common symptom during the second and third trimesters, and we were discussing various stretching exercises when Dr Derek wandered in and sat in the corner like a kid in detention.

"And how are we all feeling?" he asked in that seductive voice of his.

"Everything appears to be fine," replied the midwife on our behalf. "Just a bit of leg cramp."

"Ah, that's perfectly normal," said Dr Derek, and we nodded appreciatively. Had he said global warming was perfectly normal, we might have nodded appreciatively.

The midwife ushered my wife into the next room for an ultrasound scan and Dr Derek stood beside me by the side of the bed. I hadn't felt this star-struck since I was eleven years old when I bumped into West Ham legend and World Cup winner Martin Peters after a charity match. I went to shake his hand, panicked, went for the wrong hand—the one holding all his personal belongings—and made what could only be perceived as an amateurish attempt to mug him. The confused Peters instinctively pulled his bag away from Dagenham's youngest mugger while my mother snapped a photograph of her dumbstruck son playing tug of war with one of only two Englishmen to have ever scored in a World Cup Final.

Fortunately, I could not shake Dr Derek's hand as it was gliding across the jelly on my wife's stomach. Dr Derek is a wizard with a tube of jelly and an ultrasound machine but, like many before him, he failed to get our shy baby to perform for its audience. He tracked our baby's movements and zigzagged his way across the swollen belly, but the usually indefatigable doctor had to concede defeat after several unsuccessful attempts. We were delighted to see Dr Derek, but our baby clearly wasn't too fussed. It is not going to be the star-struck type, which will serve our child well should it ever encounter a freshly showered World Cup winner outside the men's changing room.

Saturday, 15 March

Antenatal classes have either evolved or have been falsely represented. On TV, antenatal classes usually consist of a number of plump women bouncing up and down on beanbags or beach balls, rubbing their stomachs and perfecting their deep-breathing relaxation techniques. At the very least, I expected antenatal classes to be practical, hands-on workshops that included mock births, basic nappy changing and even winding and burping. At our first antenatal class, I hadn't had the chance to hug or pat a plastic baby doll once or go anywhere near a fake female nipple, which was devastating.

Slightly perturbed, I checked online and flicked through a couple of baby books. All of them mentioned the basic ground covered during most antenatal sessions (diet, exercise, pain relief, birth options—natural vs Caesarean, breastfeeding and the telltale signs of crying/hunger/illness/dirty nappies), but they were rather sketchy on how this information should be disseminated.

Nevertheless, we arrived for our second and final full-day antenatal class eager for tips on how to calm, feed and change a screaming baby in a foreign country. As a welcome, the midwife-cum-lecturer wrote the acronym SIDS on the board and said, "Sudden Infant Death Syndrome. It can happen."

We had only been in the room fifteen minutes. Shoulders slumped as the group's eagerness dissipated. As lecture openers go, this one was a jaw-dropper. Of course, hard, and potentially traumatic, issues must be addressed, but kicking off the joyful, euphoric topic of a baby's first couple of days in the world with a discussion on Sudden Infant Death Syndrome does not make for a heart-warming introduction.

For the next half an hour, the workshop bore closer resemblance to a religious sermon than an antenatal class. There were plenty of thou shall nots and only a handful of thou shalls. Parents cannot do anything. It is truly a miracle that any of us found our way out of the caves. Do not smoke in the house or the car. Do not put a baby on a waterbed. Do not overheat the baby's room. Do not leave the cot in the same place. Do not allow the baby to sleep on its stomach. Do not throw a duvet over your sleeping baby until it is eighteen and heading off to university, and even then check the label first. And, saving the best to last, do not leave a baby on a beanbag. Who the hell is going to leave their newborn unattended on a beanbag? What kind of fuckwit shouts out to its three-week-old baby, "Now listen, Britney. I'm just going to the kitchen to cook up some smack so I've put on that TV show you like, *Big Brother*, turned up the central heating and put you face down on your favourite beanbag. All right, babe?"

By the time we reached our morning coffee break, we had addressed the mother's postnatal state and possible depression, aggression, Caesarean scars, hair loss, night sweats, sore perineum and decreased libido. I suspect that if my poor wife is struggling with the first six, then a decreased libido is going to be the least of our worries. In the tea room, my wife asked me to pass the sugar. I was genuinely surprised that she didn't want to pass her breakfast.

After the break, we discovered the secret rule of a crying baby—it will do it all the bloody time. The five major signals are hunger, a dirty nappy, tiredness, pain or the baby's too hot or too cold. This seemed to be stating the obvious. We do not expect to find our baby snivelling because Julia Roberts dies in *Steel Magnolias*.

Fortunately, we spent the rest of the morning watching another cheesy video titled *Getting to Know You*, which addressed the baby's first three months. I do not wish to make fun of the guinea pigs who willingly participate in these low-budget documentaries. After all, they share their experiences with first-time parents and their advice is invaluable. In this particular video, the kind-hearted souls clearly felt it was their civic duty to show the importance of bonding with their baby by playing "Puff the Magic Dragon" badly on an acoustic guitar. OK, it may not have been "Puff the Magic Dragon", but the tune definitely had that folksy, sandal-wearing vibe. The father was demonstrating the importance of being involved from the outset by being around, and interacting with, his child as often as possible. I seem to recall he was finger picking on the sofa while his wife breastfed and swayed gently along to the tuneless dirge. They were a lovely, righteous family. I just wouldn't want to be trapped in a lift with them.

The wide-eyed, slightly vacant, couple stressed the value of eye contact to establish a close, non-verbal relationship early on between mother and child. The mother demonstrated by eyeballing her baby at all times, even when she was cooking in the kitchen. In a surreal moment, the father held the baby up in the kitchen as its potato-chopping mother jabbered away at the confused child, gesturing with a long, serrated knife.

"You see, even as I work in the kitchen, there is still eye contact," gushed the knife-waving lunatic. "When I move, he still follows me around the room."

Well, of course he does. He's hoping that knife doesn't take his eye out.

In the afternoon, the session was all about the breast. I had not watched that many breasts on video with that many men in attendance since Gary Abbs used to get his dad's porn stash out whenever his parents went away. I am mature now, a father in the making, but that thought still crossed my mind. What if I find the images of strange women popping out their boobs arousing?

Thankfully, I didn't. No one in the room did. Breastfeeding is mesmerising, but it appeals to entirely different senses. It is a warm, comforting feeling of protectiveness, something that just feels right. Within seconds, the woman's breast had disappeared from the subconscious and was replaced by the stupendous image of the baby instinctively finding the nipple and suckling away. Mammals provide milk for their offspring. They do it rather well and have got the hang of it after several million years of practice. Watching the baby locate the nipple up close for the first time was truly beautiful (I'd seen my sister do it a dozen times but had never seen the actual connection before). Why do couples voluntarily swap this priceless opportunity to bond naturally with their child so it can bond with a tin of formula instead?

Because it can hurt. For some women, breastfeeding is excruciating. Many struggle at first until their nipples adapt. Others never get to grips with it and are often left feeling inadequate because they failed to satisfy their first maternal instinct to provide for their child. According to the video, getting the attachment right is the key for success. Preferably, the baby should be positioned nose to nipple, with the mouth guided up towards the nipple from underneath to suck in the whole of the areola.

"Looks easy enough on video, doesn't it?" I whispered chirpily to my wife.

"Piss off."

Nipples are sensitive. They need to be toughened up before they can be attacked by a voracious baby up to twelve times a day. The midwife pointed out that women can prepare their nipples for breastfeeding during the third trimester, if not earlier.

"If you're feeling confident, you can try sunbathing topless," she said brightly.

Our baby's due date is 4 June. That's a winter baby in Australia. If you take a look at any world map, only Tasmania and a few pods of whales stand between Victoria and Antarctica. If you whipped out your boobs here in early June, hardened nipples would be the least of your worries.

Other techniques include squeezing the nipples regularly or rubbing them with a scratchy towel. My wife has opted for the scratchy towel but I am not allowed to watch.

Once the breastfeeding section ended, the antenatal session petered out. My wife signed up for an additional breastfeeding class but as I am unable to lactate, I can't attend. So that was that. We were done. The next time we bump into any of our antenatal classmates will probably be on the maternity ward or in a playgroup session. There were lots of "good lucks", "all the bests" and "we'll be thinking of you both" comments when we all knew that the likelihood of us thinking of another couple's predicament while our own wife pushes a football out of her uterus was slim at best. We thanked the midwife and wandered off to the car.

There will be three of us the next time we leave this hospital.

Sunday, 16 March

Breastfeeding is dominating most of our conversations. I checked online and the World Health Organization recommends exclusive breastfeeding (no other food or drink, including water) for the first six months. Few would contest the benefits of colostrum in the first few days, but there is nothing on the market that can match the benefits of exclusive breastfeeding for the first few months either. According to WHO, however, barely one in three infants is exclusively breastfed during the first four months. There are all kinds of valid, and less valid, reasons: lack of education, it's too painful, the mother chooses to go back to work, the father feels neglected or, in one or two cases, it's just too troublesome and inconvenient.

WHO can espouse the merits of natural feeding as much as it likes, but you cannot use the maid's or the nanny's breast and there is not always a breast pump handy when you need one, is there?

I know I am being facetious and there is every possibility I could be beaten to a pulp by the I Told You So Brigade if my wife is unable to breastfeed our baby. Besides, I was raised on formula milk and it didn't do me any harm, doctor. Even though I had a vague recollection of being told I wasn't breastfed, I struggled to recall the details so I called my mother.

"No, I didn't breastfeed you," she confirmed. "But I did breastfeed your sister and I expressed the milk for your little brother."

I felt slighted initially, the disadvantaged, black sheep of the family, standing underweight and malnourished alongside my milky white siblings.

"Why did I miss out then?" I asked.

"Because, Neil, you were a little fucker."

That's a medical term. You can find it listed under the International Code of Breast-milk Substitutes section on the World Health Organization's website.

"Really? Why?"

"You were a biter. You bit me so hard, so aggressively, that it ended up being too painful. Then you didn't get enough milk so you screamed the place down in frustration because you were still hungry. I kept going for three weeks but switched to formula because you cried all the time."

My mother now admits that had my little brother behaved in a similar fashion, she would probably have persevered, but who knows?

I was a little fucker.

"For 30 years, I've lived with a mother's guilt," she continued. "You feel like you've failed. Don't beat yourself up about it if your child can't breastfeed."

That is easier said than done. In 2006, the World Health Organization set new, unambiguous benchmarks for a child's growth. For the first time, breastfeeding was referred to as the biological norm. In the United States, national campaigns told parents that breastfeeding protected babies from colds, ear infections, diarrhoea and even obesity. To possibly scare parents further, American Senator Tom Harkin, Democrat of Iowa, proposed putting warning labels on the sides of formula tins, like those on cigarette packets, pointing out that breast milk is more beneficial. The National Childbirth Trust, Save the Children and UNICEF called for similar advertising amendments in 2007 in Britain, where companies are not allowed to advertise formula milk for babies under six months. In Singapore, where I lived for a decade and two-income families are not only the norm but socially expected, I can imagine that particular campaign going down well. There are entire aisles devoted to formula in Singapore's supermarkets.

When the American Academy of Pediatrics suggests that breastfed babies are at a lower risk of Sudden Infant Death Syndrome and serious diseases such as asthma and leukaemia, then non-breastfeeding mothers are always going to feel guilty. There has even been research to suggest breastfeeding may reduce the risk of breast cancer in both mother and daughter. How does a non-breastfeeding mother come back at that?

Guilt associated with not breastfeeding permeates baby chat rooms. I clicked around and read about mums who were stigmatised by their peers because they found breastfeeding too painful or could not produce enough milk. Others breastfed but switched to formula milk too soon. There were even working mums who breastfed exclusively for two months, expressed milk for the babysitter to bottle-feed once they returned to work but found they couldn't express enough so reluctantly waved the white flag and brought in the tins. The stories were all different, but the contrition was the same—a sense of penitence that was inadvertently brought into our living room. I read out the World Health Organization's recommendations on breastfeeding to my wife and listed some of the diseases our baby would be at greater risk of catching if it takes the bottle over the boob.

"All right, Neil, that'll do," she shouted back.

"What?"

"Don't you think I'm under enough pressure? I've got all the books, the midwives and people at work telling me that I must breastfeed. Now, I've got you and the bloody World Health Organization on my back."

She was right, of course. I know my wife. She will do everything she physically can to feed our child naturally and if she can't, then she can't. And that is all there is to say about breastfeeding.

Monday, 17 March

29 weeks today. The baby's elbows are beginning to stick out as they struggle for room to manoeuvre. There is little room left in the inn and discomfort is becoming the norm for my wife. Being a petite woman anyway, the weight is centred only around her uterus making leverage a real problem. Watching her get off the sofa as if she were a flailing turtle makes us both laugh, but she is exhausted by the time she gets into an upright position. Our baby should be heading towards 1.5 kg by now, but that does

not take into account the placenta or the amniotic fluid (at least 1 litre) that is sloshing about inside. My wife's breathing is also noticeably more laboured as her expanding uterus pushes up on the diaphragm and reduces her lung capacity. She is resting more now, which gives me a chance to talk rubbish to the baby.

Research shows that with only ten or so weeks to go, babies are not only able to hear but can identify specific voices as well. It is extraordinary to think that my baby should be able to detect, deduce and store such knowledge already and I am eager to take advantage. So I have taken to talking to my wife's bump. She doesn't mind, largely because she is asleep. I prefer to chat with my baby when I go to bed, usually around 2 a.m. I sneak under the duvet and talk in whispers. The baby occasionally kicks and the euphoric rush is such an incomparable high that it feels absolute and complete until it gives way to an unexpected impatience. I want my baby now. I want to hold it now.

When the baby responds directly to its father's voice and a paternal connection is made, all rationality is overtaken by selfishness. For a few moments, I refuse to compute the risks involved if the baby were to be born ten weeks premature. I want to cuddle my firstborn. I want to squeeze my child tightly and never let go. I want my baby to be here now.

Thankfully, such irrational behaviour doesn't last. As soon as the baby settles down again and the kicking and elbowing subside, selfishness gives way to elation and I accept the importance of playing the waiting game. Besides, ten weeks will give me a chance to brush up on my small talk. The baby only needs to hear my voice regularly at the moment which is rather fortunate because my one-sided conversations in the small hours are monumentally dull. After spending most of the day sitting at a desk, I do not have the most thrilling anecdotes to share with a foetus. This evening I told my baby what I had for dinner and discussed West Ham's current form (mediocre), the plight of Tibetan protestors (very bad) and the quality of the second series of *Life on Mars* (very good). My child may one day thank me for an eclectic, well-rounded knowledge of current affairs and popular culture. My child may also call me a boring bastard.

Tuesday, 18 March

My wife's leg cramps are getting worse. What began as an occasional twinge progressed to her legs seizing up if she sat still for too long and has now reached the stage where the pain is waking her up. This is a common symptom of pregnancy, and one that becomes more prevalent, not to mention painful, in the third trimester. I've watched my wife push herself up from the sofa only to fall back down again as her thigh muscles seize in protest. Her cramping is exacerbated by the fact that she has not gained weight anywhere else. Indeed, she lost weight in the first trimester and her slender legs look ready to buckle under the strain. When she floats past the living room in the early hours of every morning to use the toilet, she does so with a limp. She bears the additional burden with typical good humour, but I do worry about her.

Thursday, 20 March

Keep glucola away from my wife. She may have the makings of an addict. Today, she went for her gestational diabetes test (or the oral glucose tolerance test), which is usually conducted between 24 and 28 weeks. We are a fraction late, but why break the habit of this pregnancy? As some women develop gestational diabetes during the latter stages of pregnancy, it has become routine to test for it. The placenta increases the levels of certain hormones produced during pregnancy which can disrupt insulin's ability to manage glucose (sugar). As a result, some pregnant women find that they have high blood sugar levels. In the United States, between 3 and 5 per cent of all pregnant women are diagnosed with gestational diabetes so it is a test worth taking

The only drawback is that my wife would be content to take the test every day. The nurse gave her a green, sugary fizzy drink (the glucola), which she promptly devoured. She then burped and had to stop herself from turning into Oliver Twist.

"That was delicious, just like limeade" she whispered. "I want some more."

As the drink generally contains around 50 g of glucose, I had to play Mr Bumble and advise against more glucola or risk dragging my hyper wife down from the ceiling. She waited an hour for her body to absorb the glucose and then had a blood sample taken. The blood test will measure how the additional glucose was processed by her body. If all is well, no follow-up will be required. If her blood glucose level is considered too high, she may have to take a second test. Either scenario would not faze my sweet-toothed partner, who plans to email pharmaceutical companies to beg them to sell glucola in supermarkets.

Monday, 24 March

30 weeks today and a minor milestone was reached last night. I had my first dream about our baby. I'm sure other parents could regale me with tales about their first dreams. I'm sure they were elaborate affairs with the baby descending from on high, via a fluffy cloud, surrounded by its loved ones. Perhaps there was

an orchestra on hand to play Beethoven's "Ode to Joy" or The Ronettes' "Be My Baby" to welcome the anointed one into the world. These kinds of panoramic, Technicolor dreams must add a spring to your step. These are the dreams that prospective parents dream of having.

In my dream, however, my baby turned into a plastic lizard. Now that cannot be good.

From what I recall, we had just had our baby in a Victorian gothic building that was a cross between St Trinian's and Wayne Manor. As there were no midwives, we had to comfort the dozens of other crying babies lying in plastic incubators on either side of a maternity ward that was hundreds of metres long. It was all a bit Brave New World so my wife's parents popped up to inject some much needed verisimilitude into proceedings. My mother-in-law patted all the babies on the left while my father-in-law shouted at all the crying babies on the right.

"For God's sake, shut up," he cried, as he marched from cot to cot. "Give it a rest, you noisy little bastards."

"Are you supposed to say that?" I called out.

"Of course I am," my father-in-law replied. "They told us to help out ... Now, shut up, the lot of you."

A quick jumpcut later and the five of us were in a cold, drab, sparsely furnished room somewhere in the decaying hospital. My in-laws were trying to light a fire with neither wood nor paper while my wife expressed concern that our baby was too quiet.

"It's not time yet," she muttered repeatedly. "It's not time yet. That's why the baby is so quiet. It's not time yet."

I took the baby from my wife and started to examine it, removing the muslins, sheets and clothes that the baby was swathed in, concealing its face. When I took off all the layers, the answer presented itself.

"That's why the baby's not crying," I said authoritatively. "It's a toy lizard."

Everything made sense now and there was a chorus of "oh yeahs" and a collective sigh of relief. I turned the plastic toy lizard over.

"Look underneath. That explains everything," I said. "The lizard was made in China."

And then I woke up sweating, but grateful that I had not spawned a fork-tongued reptile. What did all that symbolism mean? Made in China? No, it wasn't. The baby wasn't even made in Singapore. It missed out by a couple of months. The baby was made in Australia. Had Kevin Rudd's recent speeches in Mandarin and his efforts to bolster Australia-China ties seeped into my subconscious?

I checked out some of those dream interpretation websites and a couple of encyclopaedia entries on dream therapy but none of them mentioned anything about your baby turning into a toy lizard. One website did claim that dreams involving animals represent Man's primitive desires and sexual nature, but that website seemed to believe that most dreams had a sexual connotation tucked away somewhere. Judging by some of the postings on these websites, lizard dreams are more common than I initially thought but they usually involve a chase sequence (as most dreams do). A website called dreammoods.com did attempt to analyse lizard dreams specifically, claiming that the reptile may represent a person who is viewed as cold-blooded or thick-skinned. It must have taken them hours to come up with that. For the record, I do not believe my child will be cold-blooded, scaly-skinned or behave anything like an Australian Thorny Devil.

But there was one intriguing element about the dream that has stayed with me. The baby in my wife's arms was a boy.

Thursday, 27 March

I had quite a philosophical chat with my sister today. It was the birthday of her twin boys and we were discussing, as everyone does in this situation, what she was doing to ensure that her oldest son did not feel neglected. Her firstborn had a year to dominate his parents' attention before his twin brothers came along, which makes for a delicate balancing act for my sister and the evolving relationships she has with all three sons.

With my firstborn on its way, I am fascinated by birth order and its potential impact. Austrian psychiatrist Alfred Adler (1870–1937) is considered to be one of the first theorists to claim that birth order influences personality. Scientists have since debated the popular topic for over a hundred years without reaching any definite conclusions. It's not as simple as analysing the Roosevelt and the Bush families and determining that firstborns produce presidents, even if it is fascinating to note that Elliot Roosevelt died of alcoholism at the age of 34, seven years before big brother Teddy became president. Look at Serena Williams. She ended up usurping big sis Venus on the tennis court, and Napoleon was the second of eight surviving Bonapartes. So the superior firstborn argument does not always stand up.

Furthermore, the methodology required for any meaningful study is mind-boggling. To achieve any statistical data of any value, scientists need to gather huge samples of families and take into account so many random, but highly influential, factors like the number of siblings, geography, socio-economic status, religion, schooling, ethnicity, culture and even physical appearance. Will a second-born son who looks like a young Brad Pitt be automatically less confident and assertive than his big brother who looks like a bulldog chewing a wasp?

With my child about to follow in my footsteps (firstborn),

rather than my wife's (second-born), we are both curious to see which characteristics it adopts, if any. There is no doubt, unfortunately, that I dominated my little sister as she grew up. Our parents had divorced, our mother had to work and I took on the role of the household's patriarch, which is my lame attempt to justify my decision to arbitrarily cut my sister's hair one morning. She was five years old and had long flowing locks down her back. I was seven, bored and in possession of a pair of scissors. We couldn't always afford haircuts and my mother was too busy to give her daughter a trim. What's a responsible, big brother supposed to do? By the time I'd finished, my sister's butchered fringe resembled a roller-coaster track.

It works both ways. Typical characteristics of a second child include a feisty rebelliousness, and perhaps even a Bohemian side, which my younger sibling was often eager to demonstrate. I can remember thinking what a feisty little sister I had when she set the kitchen on fire one morning and stood back to admire her handiwork while the cooker melted. My mother kept calling her things beginning with "f", too.

There certainly appear to be positives by coming first. In June 2007, Norwegian researchers released a study suggesting that firstborns are smarter, with an average three-point IQ advantage over the next sibling. Some might argue that that figure is of little consequence, but it could be the difference in the firstborn getting into Cambridge or Harvard and the second child not.

Firstborns monopolise their parents' attention, gobble 100 per cent of the food available and always perform solo for an exclusive audience until their siblings come along. Their first smile, words and steps are always recorded for posterity. If the second child comes along and mimics "Singin' in the Rain", he or she will still struggle for top billing in the family household. No matter how thrilling, sequels rarely top the emotional value attached to the original. The *Empire Strikes Back* is a superior film on just about every level, but everyone remembers the first time they saw *Star Wars*. My sister was a placid, pretty little girl, but I dominate most of the early family albums, even though I looked like a heroin addict going cold turkey in most of the photographs.

Physically, mentally and emotionally nourished in many instances, firstborns supposedly wield the tools to go out and conquer. A 2008 survey of corporate heads carried out by Vistage, an international organisation of CEOs, reported that 43 per cent of the people who occupy the boardroom hot seat are firstborns. Studies have also found that the U.S. Congress is overloaded with firstborns. Our baby will certainly have a lot to live up to.

"Well it would do if all that stuff wasn't a load of rubbish," my wife said.

She has a point. My wife is fiercely independent, studied longer than her older sister and is not particularly keen on risk-taking. Risk-taking is often considered an attribute of the younger sibling who is looking for a short cut to catch up with the older sibling. My sister's educational career surpasses mine. She is more gregarious and has no problems organising fancy dress parties, which require her to dress up as Dorothy from *The Wizard of Oz*, when the mood takes her. Families are messy, with two households in the same street unlikely to share the same characteristics.

Firstborns can succeed or fail for reasons that no scientific study can reveal. George W. Bush was the firstborn Bush. John F. Kennedy was the second-born Kennedy. What does that tell you? Our child will have a firstborn father and a second-born mother. Who knows what impact, if any, that will have on the baby's personality. We can only hope that it stays away from scissors and doesn't set fire to the kitchen.

Sunday, 30 March

We cannot seem to escape horror stories involving babies being dropped or dunked. Today, a lovely lady recounted the heart-warming tale of when she dropped her newborn into the bath and dunked his head underwater. She was giving her baby his first bath when he wriggled free and slipped underwater. The baby only went under for a couple of seconds, but it was enough for the hormonal first-time mother to break down and declare she was an unfit parent. Of course she wasn't. The point she was putting across was that mistakes will be made so do not worry about it. The kind-hearted soul was trying to reassure me but I left the room positively shitting myself. I cannot bang a nail into a wall without dropping the hammer and/or the nail. What chance have I got with a wriggling, wet baby?

My mum, who enjoys a scary baby story or six, loves to recount the time I was sitting in my high chair when I lurched over suddenly, fell out of the high chair and landed on my head. Apparently, I spun around for a few, not uninteresting, seconds before collapsing in a heap. I was only six months old at the time, but if her story is genuine, I might have invented break-dancing.

Around the same time, my family was posing for photographs beside the local public swimming pool when my teenage uncle decided to drop me in in the name of science. He was not entirely sure whether newborn babies sank or floated. According to family reports, I did neither. Instead, I span around in circles on my back like a traumatised housefly.

My wife and I listen to most of these horror stories with a dollop of healthy scepticism. However, any story involving a baby being dropped, dunked or dipped, no matter how benign or innocuous, does trouble me. I do not plan to throw our child out of a high chair or test its buoyancy in a swimming pool but I am plagued with distressing images of me dropping it. Is it normal to have such fears? My paranoia is hardly something I can share with other parents. I cannot open a conversation with, "Yeah, well, the thing is, I keep seeing images of myself walking down the high street and, just like that, I drop my baby onto the pavement like a bag of potatoes."

This irrational fear will not go away. Both my wife and I are generally clumsy people, but that's a facile explanation. We are creating something unique, something that we've been moving towards for over a decade. The pregnancy feels almost too good to be true and whenever I start thinking about it, I instinctively wonder what the catch is. Where's the bump in the road? I am helping to create something special. Please God, don't let me somehow break it. The thought of holding something so precious and so perfect has assumed such an importance that I am now terrified of ever letting it go.

Monday, 31 March

31 weeks today. In the third trimester particularly, mothers-to-be can suffer from what is called "pregnancy amnesia" or "mommy brain". My wife calls it "I don't know my arse from my elbows". Pregnant women may experience short-term memory loss or general absentmindedness. Many women describe an overall feeling of distraction, which can probably be put down to the 2-kg being kicking around inside the uterus. According to a report in The Australian Journal of Advanced Nursing, an astonishing 82 per cent of women interviewed said that they had experienced some form of absentmindedness or had found it hard to concentrate during their pregnancy. There are a number of hypotheses, but no

definitive explanation for one of the more common side effects of pregnancy. Some attribute the forgetfulness to changing hormone levels, which undoubtedly fluctuate during pregnancy, but that kind of theory always strikes me as a cop out when explaining away a woman's symptoms. A woman is being forgetful. Blame it on those wretched hormones. She forgot to record my favourite TV show. Hormones! She's shagging a professional footballer and hosting cocaine parties. Hormones!

Some studies have claimed that this memory loss is due to the brain shrinking slightly during pregnancy. Others have blamed it on stress and iron deficiency. Either way, the "third-trimester fog" has descended over our household and is proving to be tremendous fun. My wife called me at the office today to complain that her lasagne was taking too long to bake and that there was clearly something wrong with the "fucking oven". She called me back five minutes later, admitting that she had forgotten to turn the "fucking oven" on. The light was on, both metaphorically and in the oven, but no one was home.

Yesterday morning, I was reading the newspaper when my wife presented herself in the living room and stared at the carpet.

"I have absolutely no idea what I came in here for," she said. I put my paper down immediately. This was much more entertaining.

"What were you doing before you came in?" I asked enthusiastically.

"I can't remember."

"Why not retrace your steps?"

"How can I retrace my steps if I don't know where the hell I was?"

"Good point," I conceded, but continued to probe the

"mommy brain". "Why don't you literally walk backwards, like a video on rewind, and see if you end up back where you started."

"Why don't you piss off?"

She eventually found her way back to the bedroom and, after examining every other item, spotted her mobile phone beside the bed and realised she had gone to the living room to get its charger. By the time she had completed the five-second journey, any recollection of charging her phone had gone and she had some difficulty remembering who I was. She now leaves notes everywhere, detailing the day's agenda and any outstanding errands or engagements in a paranoid bid to stop her mind unravelling. She is turning into Guy Pearce in *Memento*.

Tuesday, 1 April

Today I had what can only be described as a mild panic attack. We're not ready. We're not prepared. We're going to fail. My sleep patterns have become increasingly irregular, partly because my wife is still pissing for England, but mostly because I have a tendency to worry. I am about to take my first-time father test and I am not overly keen on failing.

My subconscious has been plagued by the common "sitting an examination" dream/nightmare ever since I revised for my final university exams back in 1996. Although that was over twelve years ago and characters and locations have changed since then, the basic theme doesn't. In the dream, I have always passed my exams and my life is close to my actual reality. Until I realise that I haven't actually passed my exams. My present life is nothing more than a dream within the dream and I find myself back at university preparing to take the exams. My reality is almost within reaching distance, so close it's excruciating, but I cannot seize it until I pass the pesky exams. Sometimes I am well prepared for them, sometimes I am not. Mostly I am either late for the exams or for the final year itself. Either way, my future rests only on the outcome of those university exams.

The "taking a test" dream is a universal one and hardly requires me to lie back on a leather couch and stare at a potted plant to work it out. Those exams were the launch pad for my career and, therefore, my life. Without them, I'm still living in a shitty, decrepit Victorian hovel in Manchester and surviving on £10 a week. Those exams represented my gateway, my escape route. I was the anti-Dorothy. I did not want to click my heels three times and return home. I remain the anti-Dorothy and the dream returns with a vengeance whenever I reach a crossroads.

In the last couple of weeks, my nights of fitful sleeping have taken on a surreal quality. I lie awake for an hour or so, leafing through a mental diary to allocate a time to finish off the nursery, before drifting off back to the mid-1990s, a time when Oasis was the world's biggest band and I was swotting up on the differences between Stalinism and Nazism. A couple of hours later, the woman beside me heaves her inflated frame out of the bed to empty her bladder and I briefly return to the nursery's colour scheme before my psyche takes me back to that Victorian hovel near Manchester University, a bad haircut and an intense revision schedule.

I can almost hear the clock ticking.

Wednesday, 2 April

Today was a day of incomparable productivity. I felt it was getting a bit Freudian with all that dream analysis so I decided to tackle my anxiety. Neither of us had work today so we dedicated the time to finishing our baby's kingdom. Without fail, the nursery would be ready by the end of the day.

We started the day by traipsing around every baby shop in Geelong. We came away with a baby's bath, a bouncing chair thingy and all the other accessories needed for a nursery: blankets, duvets, sheets, wall hangings, curtains, a wall border and a valance. Until this morning, I had no idea that a valance was the name of that strip of drapery that hangs along the top of curtains or around the frame of a bed. I always thought it was called "that thing across the top of the curtains or around the frame of the bed". Now that I've discovered it has a name, and a delightfully pretentious one at that, I intend to use it at every opportunity.

In the evening, we returned to the nursery to finish what we had started a couple of months ago. The cot, changing table and breastfeeding rocking chair were up. Now we had to make the place look more like a cosy nursery and less like a dentist's waiting room.

We went for an animal theme. The theme was Noah gone global. The animals went in ten by ten. They roared, hopped, swung and swum across the curtains, the wall hangings, the bedspread and, let us not forget, the valance. We were almost done. Only the border remained.

Until we moved to Australia, we lived in rented apartments so had never had the need to decorate. My experience at interior design extended to a *Star Wars* poster on the living room wall. The border was always going to be beyond my home decor capabilities. It was slippery, pre-pasted, wallpaper-type stuff and required a bucket of water, a ruler, dozens of measurements and a pair of exhausted adults to put it up. All we had to do was get the border in a straight line along the wall. It might have been easier to settle the border along the Gaza Strip. We dunked the border in the bucket of water, stretched its playful animals out along the wall and aligned it against the pencil marks. Well, when I say "we", I really mean "she". My wife wisely took charge of proceedings when I was debating whether to move the first border piece up or down a millimetre.

"Give me the bloody thing," she ordered. "Or we'll be here all night."

She dunked, stretched, placed and aligned with breathtaking efficiency. My only contribution was to offer a few ill-timed directions.

"Lower. You need to go a bit lower," I pointed out to my sweat-drenched wife, who was holding up a sopping, two-metre-long border while the paste trickled down her arms. "No, no, you've gone too far now. You need to go up just a tad, mate."

"You know what you can do with your 'tad', don't you?"

I knew what I could do with my tad. I sat in the rocking chair and watched my wife finish off the border. Marvellous woman, my wife. She stood back to examine her handiwork, wiping her brow before sticking her hands in their usual position behind her hips. She nodded slowly, clearly pleased with her efforts.

"I think there's a bit of a bubble above that monkey's head," I offered.

She turned and looked down at me but didn't utter a word. I knew what I could do with my bubble.

My mother had sent us a mobile that plays John Lennon's "Imagine" so I attached it to the cot, switched it on and we had a little dance around the finished nursery. We swayed and giggled together. It was perfect. So perfect that my wife pulled away suddenly and sat in the rocking chair. She had tears in her eyes.

"It's all right, mate," I whispered, as I crouched down and rubbed her back. "I'll fix the bubble above that monkey's head."

Sunday, 6 April

I have started jogging. Given that my wife has recently taken to sitting spreadeagled on the floor, claiming she is giving her pelvic floor muscles a workout, I thought it was the least I could do. Besides, I don't want to be Beer Belly Dad or Junk Food Dad. Parents who give birth and treat their baby's body like a temple while treating their own with contempt seem to be spectacularly missing the point. No matter how enthusiastic, a child cannot bat and bowl simultaneously. If our child fancies smacking a ball across a tennis court fifteen years from now, I hope to be physically capable of standing on the other side of the net to smack it back and batter the little bastard in straight sets.

There are plenty of websites available offering fitness tips for dads. Sites called "FitDads", "2 B Fit", "How to Exercise with the Kids" and "dads and MILFs" are all extremely helpful. Although the last one was a mistake on the part of the search engine, it is still a site that I fancy might provide ample opportunity to work up a sweat, but for entirely different reasons.

One particularly useful website offered nine ways that fathers could exercise safely with their children. Cycling, swimming, walking, volksmarching (isn't that just fast walking?), hiking and taking the toddler out in a stroller or cart were some of the more obvious tips, along with Rollerblading and rock climbing (or rather wall climbing). The tip that really stood out was titled "get down at home", and boogie, presumably. Dads were recommended to spin a couple of their favourite CDs and encourage their children to twist their melons on the living room rug. I can imagine my child's reaction when I try to coax it off the sofa by whacking on "Ice Ice Baby" and doing my white rapper's dance.

For now, I'll stick with jogging. I went for my first run last week. I made it to the end of the street, collapsed on a garden wall, clasped my stomach and checked for a bullet wound. With blurred vision and jelly legs, I wobbled home and breathlessly informed my wife that my baby would still love me if I was Beer Belly Dad.

"Of course it will. If that's what you want to do, fine," she replied. "But don't come running to me if you can't play with your children. Well, you won't be able to, will you?"

She's adept at my pressing buttons. I was back on the street the next day. Progress had been slow until tonight when I made a major breakthrough. I downloaded the *Rocky* soundtrack to my iPod. No prospective father aiming "2 B Fit" should be without it. I've been running up and down flights of steps and everything. I will be ready to go the distance by 4 June. Gonna fly now.

Monday, 7 April

32 weeks today. Most books agree that, by this stage, the lungs should have progressed to the point where they can support life. If our baby was born today, it would survive, barring any unforeseen complications. My poor wife is struggling at the moment. The once occasional backache now plagues her for most of the day. Knowing that this is a normal development in the third trimester is of no consolation. Around 50 per cent of all pregnant women experience some kind of back pain. As the baby's size increases, the additional weight of the woman's abdomen can pull the lower spine forwards, making it curved. That's where

the strain on the lower back muscles comes in, which, in turn, only adds pressure to the upper back muscles.

To try and ease the discomfort, my wife places a pillow in the driver's seat to support her lower back when she drives to work. The pillow gives her some relief, although admittedly not much. Nevertheless, I love it. In fact, I often sit in the passenger seat during short trips just to laugh at her. The pillow pushes her so close to the windscreen that she looks like she's about to be ejected. With her nose so close to the windscreen, she leaves condensation marks. It's like driving with Miss Daisy.

Tuesday, 8 April

We experienced an interesting side effect of the pregnancy this evening. My wife was laughing at my attempts to flick my underpants into the air and catch them on the back of my head when she stopped suddenly. She clutched her stomach. For a moment, she looked horrified.

Oh no.

"What's wrong?" I asked.

"I think I just wet myself," she replied and waddled past me, out of the bedroom and into the bathroom as quickly as her pregnant legs would carry her.

She had not wet herself, but it was the closest of calls. When you pee as much as she does, the spectre of stress incontinence always looms large. The pelvic floor muscles have enough to concern themselves with at the moment and a sudden increase in abdominal pressure from laughing—something my wife does a lot—may allow a few drops to squeeze through.

Being a caring husband, I am taking this additional responsibility seriously by making her laugh as often as possible.

Thursday, 10 April

We visited our favourite midwife for the monthly check-up today. She greeted us with her customary welcome of picking on me immediately.

"I see he's got that notepad with him again," she sniffed. "He's quite the scribe, isn't he?"

"Well, it's just for posterity," I mumbled.

"And how are you doing?" she continued, turning to my wife and pretty much ignoring me. She has the knack of making me feel like I am standing on a rug that someone is trying to vacuum. Every jab that she makes seems to hint at the same thing—I should do the courteous thing and bugger off so the professionals in the room can go about their business.

"Oh, I'm OK," my chirpy wife replied. "A bit of backache, but that's to be expected."

"Yeah, there's nothing we can do about that really I'm afraid," said the midwife. "Are you still working?"

"Yeah, I want to work for as long as possible and keep myself active," my wife said.

The midwife turned back to the irritant standing on her rug.

"You're a real slave driver, aren't you?"

I was stunned into silence. No witty comeback. No pithy put-down. I tucked my head into my chest and wandered behind the two women into the examination room. I think she was aiming for humour. I know what I wanted to aim for. Her joke came off wrong and, for the first time in the pregnancy, I wanted to leave the room.

I know for a fact that I am often the only man who turns up with their pregnant partner to our appointments. I am a first-time father obsessed with absorbing as much prenatal information as possible. I am venturing into the unknown. Of course there will be feelings of inadequacy, a nagging suspicion that I am somehow unprepared. This is our first time down this road. There is no precedent. I am going to feel insecure because I am taking that bloody exam again, only this time I have no idea what the questions will be. How should I know when my wife must stop work? Should she have stopped already? Should I have been more forceful? Does that make me a slave driver? All of these questions bounced around in my head as the midwife examined my wife. This is how sensitive fathers-to-be react when they are made to feel about as welcome as a fart in an astronaut's suit.

Fathers-to-be are not interfering when we enquire about our wife's weight, diet and exercise patterns. Most of the time, our only motive is our partner's welfare and the rolled eyeballs usually reserved for the thick kid in class are not always appreciated.

Friday, 11 April

The names have finally been settled. If we have a boy, he will be called Martin, as in "Peters, West Ham and England legend". If we have a girl, she will be called Polly, as in "put the kettle on".

That's it. We're done. The final names are Martin or Polly. Those two choices were the consensus after a fair and democratic process. My wife's kindergarten kids picked them. After brainstorming various options (including Thomas, Percy and Bob or Dora, Hannah and Montana), the class voted on their choices, agreed on Martin and Polly and insisted that no other alternatives will be entertained at this late stage.

Saturday, 12 April

There is one name that we have been toying with for some time but were reluctant to go public with for one extremely pertinent reason. We are not sure if it is a name.

We are infatuated with the name "Addis".

Our baby Addis.

Addis Humphreys.

Cute little Addis.

We have been struggling with girls' names for some time. No common ground is shared on this issue. Discussions became so petulant that, at one point, I refused to consider any name other than Ivana, promising to forever pronounce our daughter's name "Ivana Hump Free". Boys' names have not really been an issue. We love any number of the interwar, two-syllable, street urchin names like Charlie, Billy, Harry, Alfie and Johnny. Real boys' names for real boys. But we have hit a brick wall with the girls. In an attempt to get somewhere, we ventured down the interwar route, only to end up with bunches of flowers.

"There is Rose, Lily, Daisy and Violet," my wife said to me recently.

"Yeah, I know, but you've named half my aunties right there," I replied. "Besides if we're going to go with flowers, then they should at least be native Australian flowers."

"Like what?"

"I don't know. How about bottlebrush?"

"How about sod off?"

We continued to go round in circles. Then Addis suddenly popped up from nowhere. Well, not quite from nowhere, it appeared through our windscreen. Point Addis is one of our favourite Australian locations. Tucked between the famous surfing destination of Bells Beach near Torquay and the coastal town of Anglesea further along the Great Ocean Road, Point Addis is blessed with rugged sandstone cliffs that overlook the Bass Strait. The panoramic views are both breathtaking and humbling. It is home to a marine national park, where whales occasionally pop by in season, while the overlooking forest hosts kangaroos, wallabies and my best monotreme mate, the echidna. It is hardly surprising that the area is sacred to the local Aborigines. Point Addis is not far from where we live and we have trekked and picnicked around the forest many times.

We love Point Addis ... Addis ... The more we thought about it, the more it sounded like a cute name for a baby girl. Our little baby Addis. If Brooklyn was good enough for the Beckhams, then the prehistoric, natural beauty of Point Addis was certainly good enough for the Humphreys.

The connotations were obvious, according to our parents.

"You weren't shagging up there, were you?" my father-in-law asked. "You'd freeze your balls off up there."

"No, of course not," I replied.

"But you said it was like Brooklyn and the Beckhams," my mother-in-law interjected.

"Yes, but not exactly like the Beckhams."

When I discussed the name with my mother, she was even more abrupt.

"I don't want my granddaughter named after a dustpan and brush set," she said.

She had a point.

I knew the word "Addis" was locked away in my subconscious somewhere. Trust my mother to find the key. Addis was written on the side of a toothbrush that I had when I was a kid. An Internet search brought all the childhood memories flooding back. Addis is a British plastics company that churns out everything from toothbrushes to brooms, mops, kitchen dustbins and my mother's dustpan and brush set. According to the company's website, its founder, William Addis, invented the first mass-produced toothbrush in 1780. How a tiny corner of a forest in Victoria at the southern end of Australia ended up sharing Mr Toothbrush's name remains a mystery. After some preliminary research into the area's history, I'm still none the wiser and, after my mother's untimely intervention, I may prefer to keep it that way. I wasn't overly keen on naming a daughter after a flower. I'm even less keen on naming her after a toilet brush.

Monday, 14 April

33 weeks today. Our baby's mother is going about her harvesting business quite nicely, so I feel the need to overcompensate for my biological irrelevance (at this stage) by reverting to my prehistoric hunter-gatherer role. I am taking on more work than I ordinarily would, working seven days a week to establish a nest egg for my firstborn. In a reversal of the sexes, I also appear to be nesting. I do not know what else to call it. I'm doing odd jobs and carrying out one or two major renovations around the house in preparation for a baby who will neither need nor appreciate them until it is at least a year old. Space has been set aside for its bulky toys and designated playing areas have been laid out around the house. I know this is anal but helping to build our baby's nest is reassuring and necessary. It makes me feel involved. As my poor wife wheezes when she gets up from the sofa, which now takes anything from five seconds to a fortnight, I busy myself with "baby tasks" that are neither urgent nor important right now. I have to do something. Anything.

Friday, 18 April

My wife did very well today. She returned home with five baby bonnets and three pairs of booties in neutral colours—naturally—and proudly told me that each cost $1 in a sale. While she was shopping, she waddled past a baby in a buggy. Communicating in the universal language used only by mothers and mothers-to-be, my wife smiled affectionately at the baby while rubbing her own stomach and the mother reciprocated with a knowing nod and a smile back at the belly.

"The baby was hilarious," my wife recalled. "She had about four hairs on her head, which were all pulled together and clipped in this awful bow. It was brilliant."

Why do parents do this? In Singapore, I recall countless Asian babies lumbered with mad parents who insisted on dragging their child's half a dozen hairs in either direction to tie a couple of straggly bunches. The babies always looked like alopecia victims.

Still babies and toddlers in Singapore were pretty much what they should be—babies and toddlers. And they were dressed as such, with babies in those light, airy one-piece bodysuits ideal for the humid equatorial climate and toddlers in little two-piece Power Rangers sets. And so was I at their age. With two-tone, stripy, knee-high socks and shorts and a Fonzie vest telling the world I was "coolamundo", I was the ace face of my kindergarten. In fashion terms, I was a child of my time.

The child of our time is difficult to pin down because, in fashion terms, today's child does not exist. The average baby and toddler are not targeted by the various clothing empires, but babies and toddlers who want to dress like thong-wearing Bratz dolls and gangsta rappers are increasingly spoilt for choice. Of course, children do not know that they want to dress like Paris Hilton or 50 Cent. They want to wear anything that allows them to smear the ice cream of their choice around their face, neck and chest.

Kids understand neither the concept of fashion nor the social importance of designer labels. If they did, they would never pee down the front of their 501s. Fortunately, they have parents to make their clothing choices for them and those high on credit cards, but low on IQ, know the score. Get the right house, postcode and car and then get the right child. That way, if you get the right child, you can wear it as a fashion accessory. The child then becomes a part of the whole tacky, superficial ensemble for cashed-up parents to display at weddings, christenings and any other social venue that still allows children and alcohol under the same roof. Some may even go the whole hog and splash out on the Gucci baby carrier so they can tell friends, "Yes, I had to go Gucci. When I saw Gwen Stefani had one, I knew I had to buy one immediately, didn't we darling? ... Right, we've done the baby. Now show them your new car."

This is nothing new. Transparent social snobbery existed among parents at my working-class comprehensive school in England, perhaps even more so (on a council estate, it is easy to pick out those who have no money because they always dress like they do). Children had to have Björn Borg's latest Fila tracksuit or John McEnroe's Nikes or else life would be an interminable hell. But they never tried to pass them off as hot or sexually arousing. Only paedophiles thought that way. In the 1980s, anyone who tried to sell the idea of sexuality to children was usually known to the local constabulary. Today, he probably gets an expense account, a company car and eats out on the story of how he brought down Barbie.

In Britain, the ageing Barbie has been knocked off her best-selling doll perch by Bratz. If Barbie was the wholesome blonde who promised nothing more than a peck on the cheek, then Bratz is her insecure, promiscuous little sister who shags the school's Neanderthal in the toilets. The Bratz girls are "hot" in cropped tops and high heels. They are pitched at precocious tweenagers who mostly think the dolls are "pretty" and want to dress like them. They lack the social awareness to tell the difference.

Thankfully, they have parents who can differentiate between "hot" and "pretty" and no self-respecting mother wants their prepubescent daughter to be "hot". So we can only wonder who buys and dresses those poor children in T-shirts with slogans like "my mum's hot" (which veers disturbingly into MILF territory), "muthasucker" and "so many boys, so little time".

Maybe I'm a grumpy old bastard. Maybe it's only a bit of a fun. Why can't a five-year-old girl wear a T-shirt that makes fun of her so-called promiscuity? She cannot be sexually active. She's only five so she can't be promiscuous. It's just a joke. Get it? Can't you see how ironic and witty the girl's parents are? Watch how those hip parents stop laughing when their innocent little girl does become a sexually active teenager desperate to be hot and sexy, as seen on her T-shirt. Such clothes send some confusing, sexualised messages to both her and the boys in the playground. And what if she doesn't live up to the billing? Imagine if cute, cuddly mini-me Paris Hilton in the playground doesn't grow into sexy, teenage Paris Hilton hanging around outside McDonalds. There will be some hormonal, teenage angst and self-esteem issues for the trendy, T-shirt-buying parents to deal with.

For that reason alone, I find the current trends in children's fashions to be so surprising. I know, as every parent knows, that my child will be an insufferable pain in the arse when it eventually leaves its brain at the door marked "puberty". At that moment, I will be rendered obsolete. Dad will cease to exist. Moron will take his place. A moron who has never been cool, never followed the latest musical trends, never got drunk, never sat an exam, never kissed a girl and never been in love. Moron has never done anything of note or value in his life. Ever. Teenage hormones will replace wide-eyed innocence with irritating sarcastic cynicism. It is inevitable. So why any parent might be in a hurry for that day to come around any faster is hard to fathom. Surely, we all want our children to remain children for as long as possible.

We hope our baby can be just a baby, not a babe, comfortable in its $1-bonnets and white towelling sets. When I picture our toddler running towards me two years from now, the only designer label I see it wearing is Häagen-Dazs.

Monday, 21 April

34 weeks today. Most books claim that long-distance travel is no longer advisable, particularly by sea or air. If there are any mothers-to-be out there booking themselves seats on round-the-world cruises six weeks before their due date, then I suspect they need medical attention for entirely different reasons. From here on in, we must seek advice from our obstetrician if we need to make any journeys of considerable distance. Yesterday, the furthest my wife travelled was from the living room to the bathroom and back.

Thursday, 24 April

Why do routine midwife appointments have a tendency to turn into a nightmare? The appointment began in the usual fashion with the handing over of the urine sample, a little giggle and a well-worn joke about its contents. I suffered the usual put-downs which I no longer believe are reserved for all men who dare to accompany their partners to these appointments. I think they're all saved up for me. She kicked off with the regular "Ooh, he's got that notepad again" and progressed to "He's hard to please" and "What's he going on about now?". Smiling through gritted teeth, I laughed at the inane jibes while my wife stretched out on the bed for some routine poking and prodding.

The midwife produced her measuring tape and stretched it across my wife's belly, which looked enormous to me.

"Hmm, not much growth there this week," she muttered.

She read some notes and then returned to my wife.

"Let's have a look at that again," she said, and lined up the cold measuring tape from one end of the bump to the other. "There doesn't seem to be any growth at all."

"Is that a problem?" I asked.

"No, I wouldn't have thought so. It's probably nothing."

Then why did you bring it up then?

"Just to put all our minds at rest, I think you should go for another ultrasound scan. Everything should be fine but I can't see any growth since your last visit two weeks ago."

My wife started to cry.

People mean well. They take a genuine interest in another person's pregnancy, most of the time. There will always be the bitter and twisted types who take the opportunity to snipe, but that is to be expected. Everyone else is legitimately concerned about the health of mother and baby. However, there is a fine line between concern and paranoia. In my wife's case, that fine line is probably between 5 and 10 kg. She has gained hardly any weight throughout the pregnancy, often as little as 0.5 kg between fortnightly appointments. Since the end of the first trimester, the numbers have always gone in the right direction, but not by much. Many pregnant women would probably be relieved to have what my mother calls "skinny genes".

Everyone knows, and I feel like a broken record here, that as long as mummy is eating, drinking, resting and exercising in the appropriate quantities, baby will get all it needs in its sterile sanctuary. Most intelligent people know this. Most thick people know this. And yet there have been times, a number of times to be truthful, when my wife has been made to feel inadequate or neglectful. Thanks to the "kindly concern" of others (i.e. busybodies), she has even entertained thoughts of being the proverbial "bad mother".

"You're not very big, are you?" friends, relatives and strangers have all said in the last couple of months.

"No, but I've always been a small person."

"Are you eating enough? You should really be getting more meat, green leafy vegetables, meat, iron tablets, meat, vitamins and meat into your body, you know."

"I'm trying to eat as much as I can."

"But you're still so small. You're *tiny*."

These comments usually come from women. Some even appear to take perverse pleasure in emphasising my wife's so-called physical deficiency.

"But you're so *tiny*," they say, accentuating the first syllable on "tiny" with a sudden high-pitched inflection change. "You're just so *tiny*. Look at you. How many months are you now?"

"Just over seven and a half months now."

"Really? Are you sure?"

No, dickhead, we're really only three months but we failed maths at school.

"Yeah, I'm definitely seven and a half months."

"No, really? But look at you. You're so *tiny*."

Annoying? Try standing in front of the melodramatic person repeating herself as she points disapprovingly at your partner's belly. It is a real struggle to resist the urge to rip out her tongue and throw it at her.

Whether their motives are caring or callous, other people almost take ownership of your pregnancy. They try to assume control as they bark orders at you incessantly: eat more, eat less; drink more, drink less; work more, work less; sleep more, sleep less; pee more, pee less. Not only do these commands come from overbearing "experts" (some of whom have never even had a baby, which I find staggeringly arrogant), they can also come with a hint of disapproval. You are underweight. You are seven months pregnant and clearly underweight. Surely you realise this? Why haven't you done something about it? And you're vegetarian, too? My God, do social services know about this? Thank God, I came along to point out the error of your ways or you'd be well and truly screwed.

For over a month now, my wife has been made to question her dietary choices and eating habits at least once a day, every day. The poor woman is mentally exhausted. I know that she is at breaking point. The midwife's concern, though benign, was all she needed.

Holding my wife's hand, I asked the midwife to book us in for the ultrasound scan immediately. I wanted to allay my wife's fears and convince her that her guilt was unwarranted. I was certain that the baby would be fine. Luckily, the ultrasound scanning centre could squeeze us in within a couple of hours so we spent the longest lunch break of our lives wandering aimlessly around the town centre, making small talk that neither of us was really listening to.

We were invited into the scanning room by an accommodating Welsh sonographer.

"Ah, right, you just want to check on the baby's weight and size then, do you?" she asked brightly, in that uplifting sing-song Welsh lilt.

"Er, yes, that's right," I said, replying on behalf of my silent wife whose apprehension was palpable in the tiny room.

"I'm not worried at all. I think the baby's fine," I jabbered nervously, trying far too hard to avoid any awkward silences. "But the size of the belly has been brought up, so we thought we should get this done for peace of mind."

"And that's exactly what it is," replied the cheery woman. "Peace of mind."

The nightmare morphed into a dream almost immediately. The thing that appeared on the screen wasn't the fragile being we had witnessed at our previous meetings, it was a fat little bastard. Our child has a discernible line of fat around its face and even has its father's chubby hamster cheeks. Now I was fighting back the tears. Tears of relief. Every major limb and organ was measured and every one of them measured up to expectations, nothing too drastic either way. Its size was just right, too. According to the sonographer's calculations, the baby was around 2.3 kg (5 lbs 4 oz). I burst out laughing. Six weeks to go and we already have a five-pounder kicking around its mother's uterus.

The day ended on a glorious high. Sitting here now, I think the midwife's professional efficiency proved to be a blessing. I never doubted the baby's size and general health, but the confirmation that the scan brought has finally, for once and for all, removed the ball and chain that my wife has dragged through the third trimester. Tiny or not, both mother and baby are fine. Pregnant women in a similar position would do well to organise a scan at this stage to determine the baby's size and condition. The scan may cost a few bucks, but peace of mind is priceless.

Sunday, 27 April

My wife keeps throwing up potential baby names from the American West.

"How about Billy Bob?" she asked this afternoon.

"As in Billy Bob Thornton?" I replied incredulously.

"Yes."

"No."

"Oh."

A pause.

"How about Betsy Lou for a girl?" she asked brightly.

"You're kidding me, right?"

"No. What's wrong with Betsy Lou?"

"What's wrong with it? ... Betsy Lou and Billy Bob?"

"Yeah. I think they're cute little names."

"Do we look like *The Waltons*?"

I love my wife. But if she thinks I'm going to wander around the house shouting, "Betsy Lou, where are you?", she's got another thing coming.

Monday, 28 April

35 weeks today. Contrary to the midwife's belief, my wife's bloated belly continues to swell and her uterus has hit the bottom of her ribcage. This is not pleasant. She fidgets more in her sleep, no position is comfortable for more than a few minutes at a time and her strangely arousing groans accompany every move she makes. Bending over is a constant problem as my wife pointed

out with a startling analogy.

"Do you remember when we took my mum and dad to see the dolphins in Port Phillip Bay?" she asked.

"Yeah."

"And my dad couldn't lean over his beer belly to put his flippers on properly?"

"Yeah."

"That's exactly how it feels when I try to put on my comfy shoes."

All of this stuff will be familiar to anyone who has glanced through a pregnancy book. The discomfort, the swelling, the tossing and turning, the difficulties maintaining balance—they are de rigueur for any how-to pregnancy guide. What they do not tell you, and what no one has ever told me, is that you have to cut your wife's toenails.

"Here, can I ask you something?" my wife asked. "Will you cut my toenails?"

I laughed.

"Yeah, sure. No problem."

"I'm serious."

"Are ya?"

"Yeah."

"Oh."

With the utmost reluctance, I agreed to cut her toenails. They didn't mention that in the antenatal classes.

Monday, 5 May

36 weeks today. Our baby should be as long as a rolled-up newspaper.

I called my wife during her lunch hour and immediately started to panic when she failed to answer. Should I return home?

Should I call Dr Derek? Should I call the hospital? We have less than a month to go. My wife could have easily … no, don't even go there. She would have called, wouldn't she? She's become so scatterbrained lately, who knows? Something must have happened. This was all her fault. After all, no one is going to hand her a gold star for working as close to the due date as possible. I've told her that as well. She reminded me that she did not lay bricks for a living. I reminded her that we had neurotic relatives on our backs who had insisted that women stopped working within five minutes of conceiving back in the 1970s.

Then, just like in the movies, the phone rang.

"Hello? Oh, it's you!" I bellowed in that toxic mix of anger and relief. "Where the hell have you been?"

"You know where I've been, Neil," my wife whispered. "I went to the clinic for a vaginal swab. I'm sitting outside waiting for the results. When you called, the bloody phone went off while the nurse was poking around up there with a cotton bud."

Oh, yeah. The vaginal swab. I'd forgotten all about that.

My acute sense of helplessness is peaking now, along with my wife's overall discomfort. I have always maintained a healthy and logical relationship towards pain. I prefer pain that I can actually see or rationalise. I've had a broken ankle, a nasty cut with a bread knife and a rusty nail through the foot, but the pain associated with each of these injuries didn't particularly bother me. I could see it, identify it and justify it. No problem. But I am no "I ain't got time to bleed" kind of guy. If the pain is invisible or irrational, I bleat like Little Bo Peep. If I sustain a migraine for long periods, I have a brain tumour. If I suffer from a protracted stomachache that I cannot explain, I have an ulcer. Good, old-fashioned cuts, breaks and bruises are my kind of injuries. What lies beneath scares the shit out of me.

I've applied my pain rationale to my wife. As we near the end of the maximum growth phase, any symptoms that I deem within the parameters of pregnancy are par for the course. Any pains that I consider outside of the parameters of pregnancy are a cause for consternation. There is a flaw in this otherwise sensible thinking. I am not a doctor and I have no idea what I am talking about.

If we're lying in bed and she so much as groans, I leap up and reach for the nearest pregnancy book. If she holds her belly and winces, I begin dialling the hospital. Fortunately, I am not alone. According to the sublime work of Ross D. Parke and Armin A. Brott in *Throwaway Dads*, expectant fathers can experience "sympathetic pregnancy". Sympathetic pregnancy, sometimes known as Couvade syndrome (from the French word meaning "to hatch"), is extremely common among expectant dads, up to 80 per cent of men suffer from it, and yet it is often dismissed as abnormal, unmanly or downright girly. Women have hormones to explain their erratic emotional state during pregnancy. What's a man's excuse? The truth is they do not need one. My wife and I have been together for sixteen years and she had never taken sick leave until the first trimester of her pregnancy. Her general physical fortitude and emotional strength have always been formidable. Now she groans every time she sits up, lies down, stands up, rolls on her side or struggles out of bed. Naturally, I react accordingly—I turn into mother hen. As her partner, I fret over her medical condition. I would be a misogynistic, self-centred bastard if I didn't.

There is a fine line between being empathetic and being an irrational drama queen. My wife and I are both nursing common colds. So I fussed around, ordered her to rest and force-fed her some vegetable soup before packing her off to bed. While I tucked her in, she said, "I appreciate what you're doing but pregnant women get colds. You don't always have to panic."

"I'm only trying to help, you miserable old cow."

"But you can't jump every time someone coughs. If you do, the baby will latch onto it and run rings around you. Remember how you reacted when you thought your little brother was sick."

Oh, I remember the time my little brother fell sick when he was under my care all right—the devious little bastard.

After his near-miraculous recovery from several life-threatening conditions as a result of his complicated birth, my little brother defied expectations and grew into the cutest toddler I had ever seen. Now I know that relatives always say this. No baby is ever ugly to its loving parents and no child is anything other than cuddly and adorable to its extended family. We've all been at family gatherings where someone pipes up and says, "Have you met John and Susan's boy? Oh, you must see him, he's the cutest baby." Then little Igor is carried out from a darkened dungeon.

"He looks like a famous film star, doesn't he?" someone will gush.

Yes, Quasimodo, you think to yourself.

"Here, you must hold little Igor," another relative will cry while John and Susan remove his manacles. "He should be fine with you. He did bite Carrie's girl, Christine, but she should have remembered that Igor really doesn't like nursery rhymes."

So you take Igor, cover his horns with a muslin wrap, pose for a family snap and pray that no one starts singing "Humpty Dumpty".

Having said that, my little brother really was different. I have never seen a little boy melt more female hearts than my four-year-old brother. Everyone wanted to spend time with him and I was no different. When I returned home from university one summer, my now-wife and I took him to see *Toy Story* at the cinema.

We never made it to the cinema. We barely made it out of the street. I turned to check on my brother in the back seat and was alarmed by his ghostly pallor. His generally pale complexion was a side effect of the hypoglycaemia. Although the condition was under control by this stage, a drop in his glucose level could lead to sudden lethargy.

"Are you all right, mate?" I asked.

He didn't answer.

"Hey? It's rude to ignore your big brother. Do you want a drink?"

His eyes appeared to glaze over and his head drooped to one side. Luckily, I am not one to panic in such circumstances.

"Turn the fucking car round now," I shouted. "He's having a fit. Get him home now!"

"How do you know he's having a fit?" my ever-so-astute wife asked. "He was fine just now."

"Just turn around and get him to mum now. She's got some medication. Move!"

Well, my poor wife took evasive action and swung the car around with a ferocity that served its purpose. We stopped only for traffic lights, and even then with extreme reluctance, hovered precariously around the speed limit and narrowly avoided a pensioner walking across a zebra crossing in the town centre. As we pulled up outside my house, I threw myself out of the car while it was still moving, wrenched open the back door, grabbed my brother in a fireman's carry and dashed towards the front door.

"Mum, he's fitting! He's fitting," I screamed. "He's fitting, mum. He's fitting."

Like a scene from *A Hard Day's Night*, several front doors belonging to several red-bricked terrace houses opened simultaneously to enjoy a bit of live entertainment.

"What are you going on about?" my mother replied, the last person in the street to open her front door.

"He's fitting, mum. He's fitting," I cried, leaping over the garden gate. "Get his medication and I'll call an ambulance. He's fitting!"

I lowered my brother onto the living room floor and watched him nonchalantly reach over for his Thomas the Tank Engine trains and start pushing them along the carpet.

"There's nothing wrong with him," said my mother.

"You made me speed through Dagenham and Barking for nothing," said my wife.

"Choo, choo," said my brother.

He was not having a fit. Nor was his sugar level particularly low. He was suffering from a mild case of car sickness which he exaggerated because—as my mother later pointed out—he was reluctant to go to the cinema in the first place after she had pulled him away from a particularly engrossing storyline on his *Thomas the Tank Engine* video. There was a lesson to be learnt that day and, in my hysteria, I failed to learn it. I still overreact and mollycoddle loved ones.

I can almost hear our baby rubbing its hands together.

Thursday, 8 May

The midwife was just fabulous today. Chatty and smiley, she complimented my wife's radiant appearance and was quick to point out that her bump had grown a couple of centimetres.

Appearing from nowhere, Dr Derek glided across the carpet and invited me to feel my baby's head. Using my thumb and forefinger, I pressed down just above the cervix in a surreal attempt to feel my firstborn's head.

"The baby's head is down and in the perfect position," Dr Derek said. "No, no, you've got to press harder."

I pretended to press harder.

"Oh, yes," I cried. "My God, it's my baby's head."

It wasn't. Pushing down clumsily on my wife's uterus seemed too risky and I chickened out.

"That's your baby's head right there," Dr Derek gushed.

"Hmm, great," I replied, not wishing to rain on his parade.

Dr Derek and the midwife returned to the room next door while my wife got off the bed and pulled up her trousers.

"You didn't feel a thing, did you?" she asked as she readjusted her maternity trousers.

"Nope."

"I knew it."

Back in Dr Derek's cosy room, the midwife handed us an antenatal card which we must present at the hospital when D-Day comes. The card documented routine medical facts, such as my wife's age, height and weight, and some details about our pregnancy. In a section headed "Notes", a midwife had handwritten "wife—vegetarian" and "husband—author".

It was the only scribble that made reference to the father. What was its relevance? Perhaps the tools of my profession will be of some service during the birth. Perhaps Dr Derek's head will pop up at the end of the bed and shout, "We need to get this little baby out now. I need a clamp, a pair of scissors and a couple of funny paragraphs."

Monday, 12 May

37 weeks today. We hadn't played it for a couple of weeks so we had a quick game of Name That Sex tonight. The string on a ring was our designated old wives' tale. My wife tied her wedding ring to the string, held it above her belly and started swinging the string.

"What's that going to prove?" I asked.

"Well, if the string moves in a circle, we're having a girl. If it stays in a straight line, it's a boy. No, wait. It's the other way round, I think."

"It doesn't matter anyway. The bloody thing is doing both."

"Yeah, it is, isn't it?"

That particular old wives' tale has certainly cleared up the gender issue. We are having a hermaphrodite.

Tuesday, 13 May

Something did not feel right. I was lying down beside my wife when I felt the baby kick. This in itself was not unusual. I often touch my sleeping wife's belly to feel around for any movements until she wakes up, groans at me and waddles off for a pee. The baby's kicking was not random; it was rhythmic and disconcertingly so. Every few seconds, the baby lashed out quite violently against the left side of my wife's uterus and then stopped abruptly. Demonstrating my characteristic imperturbability in such situations, I shook my wife and cried, "It's fitting! It's fitting!"

"What's going on?" she mumbled, rubbing her eyes.

"It's fitting. The baby's fitting. Feel it for yourself."

I grabbed my wife's left hand, probed around the left side of her swollen tummy and pinpointed the consistent pounding.

"There ... you see? Can you feel it?" I asked, my voice still rising. "It's fitting. Should we call the midwives at the hospital?"

"No, I'll think we'll be fine, Neil," she replied. "The baby's got hiccups."

I am going to be more of a hindrance than a help at the birth.

Wednesday, 14 May

My wife and I are destined to become miserable bastards. Our baby will have us singing the blues and slitting our wrists, according to Daniel Gilbert, a psychology professor at Harvard University. He was in Sydney a couple of days ago to speak at the Happiness and its Causes conference. Professor Gilbert suggested that the traditional notion of marriage bringing joy is valid, but the idea that bringing children into the relationship increases a couple's happiness does not stand up to scientific scrutiny. What's more, Professor Gilbert believes that the more kids you have, the sadder you are likely to be. Citing U.S. and European studies, he explained that a person's happiness does increase when a child is on the way but plummets rapidly after the birth. We can expect our depression to bottom out during those wondrous "hoodie" years called puberty. Professor Gilbert went on to say that a married couple's happiness does not return to its pre-child levels until their children leave home. Marriage without kids, it seems, leads to bliss.

Not surprisingly, his comments quickly travelled around the world. How can Professor Gilbert say such things? It borders on biological blasphemy, doesn't it? Evolution dictates that we are programmed to procreate. How could it be otherwise? That was certainly my knee-jerk reaction. Being present at the birth, the baby's first words, the first steps, the first day at school, the first job, first partner, marriage and grandchildren, each of these milestones brings such an emotional high that is surely impossible to replicate elsewhere. Then I thought about the flip side. When babies walk, they fall over and parents spend the next few years doing decent impressions of Boris Karloff, chasing after their tumbling children with outstretched arms. When kids talk, they argue. When they attend school, they face bullies or bully others. They stress over the pursuit of academic success or the humiliation of failure. They also cost money, hundreds of thousands of dollars. Then they find partners and, immediately, loyalties are divided and apron strings stretched to breaking point. All the while, the parents literally mop up the blood, sweat and tears and insist that they have never been happier.

Following Professor Gilbert's speech, subsequent articles popped up highlighting studies that backed his claims. According to research in Holland in the 1990s, couples with two children were less happy than those with none. Psychologists spoke of couples with children being less satisfied with their marriage than those without children. Kids cause headaches, anxious days, sleepless nights and countless marital rows and disagreements. How can that lot make parents smile?

I understood Professor Gilbert's hypothesis from a logical standpoint. It makes perfect sense. I chewed it over for a while and concluded that the argument is a load of bollocks because there is nothing logical about having children. They take up all of your time and often deprive the household of at least one salary, require massive financial investment with zero return and drain all emotional resources during the teenage years before possibly telling you where to go sometime after their sixteenth birthday because they are meeting a man from the motor trade.

I don't need the results from a psychology study to tell me that a parent's happiness index drops when her beloved boy's balls drop. I only have to recall the relationship with my mother during puberty to be reminded of that revelation. But the need to measure a parent's happiness and the pervading cynicism says more about our impatience than anything about our children. We want a fancy house now. Can't afford it? Sod it, get a hefty mortgage. We want a flat-screen TV now. Can't afford it? Sod it, stick it on the credit card. We want to be happy now. Can't be happy with kids? Sod it, we'll get a puppy instead. Why wait or work for something when we can have it now. Ignoring the nonsense of a happiness index (I can picture my grandmother's reaction had she been asked to fill in a happiness index survey as she sifted through the rubble of her bombed house during the Blitz), we are left with the most obvious of truths. Children are a sacrifice. They always have been. Why should it be any different for my pampered generation? We have satellite navigation systems in our cars, dishwashers in our kitchens, pre-programmed DVD recorders in our living rooms and a dozen other short cuts to boost our happiness. Children remain the one possession that is not, and never can be, a labour-saving device.

I think we will manage.

Thursday, 15 May

A new midwife shocked us today. After carrying out the weekly blood pressure/weight/urine test routine, we played Name That Date. The due date is 4 June. I suspect that the baby will poke its head out a couple of days earlier, on 2 June. My masochistic wife said no earlier than 11 June. The midwife laughed.

"There's not much chance of that happening," she said.

"Really?" my shocked wife replied. "What makes you say that?"

"You're running out of room. I reckon it'll be quite a bit earlier than that. I'd say 30 May."

"That's fifteen days away," I exclaimed.

We are now talking in days. Oh shit.

Friday, 16 May

My brave, but stubborn, partner finally bid farewell to her kindergarten kids today. For totally selfish reasons, I am very relieved. It has been something of a juggling act on my part. On the one hand, I did not want to play 1950s Man and order my wife to play housewife moments after conceiving last year. The decisions to continue working and when to stop are hers alone. However, recently, the pressure on me has become relentless. Whenever friends have asked how my wife is coping and I've mentioned that she is still working, they fix me with a contemptuous glare that suggests I've just spat in their eye.

"Your wife is still working. Really?" they exclaim theatrically, going all Meryl Streep on me.

"Yeah, but she's stopping soon."

"It's too late now. She's doomed. Pregnant women who work into their eighth month will surely die."

My wife is a passionate, gifted teacher who knows the physical demands of her job and the toll it takes on her body. But even she has finally admitted that now is the time to stop. For the last few days, she has returned home, flopped onto the sofa and fallen asleep almost immediately.

I want to be as sensitive as the next SNAG, but there have

been several recent discussions that have kicked off with me shouting, "Stop being a bloody hero and leave work now" and ended with me shouting, "If you want to keep working, then that's up to you, but don't blame me if anything goes wrong."

It's a nasty, tactless thing to say but I have been desperately trying to push her buttons

Fortunately, everyone can sleep soundly tonight because my wife has called it a day and received a number of gifts to mark the occasion. My favourite, off-the-wall present came from a colleague who compiled a baby-themed CD with track titles related to giving birth. The CD kicks off with the more obvious "Be My Baby", "Sweet Child of Mine", "Ice Ice Baby" and "Hit Me, Baby, One More Time". Then we've got "The Final Countdown" and "Under Pressure" before culminating with "Push It". I may play that song during the birthing process to encourage my wife.

Ah, push it. Push it real good.

Saturday, 17 May

We had the baby's car seat fitted today. The law in Australia recommends that it should be fitted by a mechanic, which is understandable in a country that has a shocking annual death toll on its roads. According to the Royal Automobile Club of Victoria, the law in Victoria states that babies under one year must be transported in an approved child restraint and passengers under sixteen must be restrained in an approved child restraint that meets with Australian standards, which all sounds reasonable. When I lived in Singapore, I can recall being in cars where unrestrained children stood up in the back, leant over the driver's shoulder and adjusted the volume of the stereo by pressing a button on the steering wheel. Was the child unsafe in the car? We were all bloody unsafe in the car. Sadly, as I write this, Singapore's authorities are still debating the merits of implementing seat belts on school buses (and weighing up the costs involved, naturally) following the recent, tragic death of an eight-year-old boy who was thrown out of a school van in a traffic accident. Bus operators have argued that they may have to charge more if such a rule is passed. So what?

In Australia, the laws regarding child restraints in vehicles are about to get tougher. New child restraint laws have recently been approved by Australia's transport ministers. When implemented, babies less than six months old must be restrained in a rearward-facing restraint, those between six months and four years need rearward- or forward-facing restraints and kids between four and seven must be secured in a forward-facing restraint or a booster. On top of this, no one below the age of seven can sit in the front seat. The RACV goes even further, recommending that children under twelve should still sit in the back.

According to our chatty child restraint fitter, not every Australian adheres to the law.

"They just arrested some bloke up in the Northern Territory," he said, while adjusting the belt strap in the back seat. "The police pulled him over and found that he had a slab of beer and a five-year-old boy in the back. And the bastard had put his seat belt around the beer and not the boy."

"You're kidding, right?" I asked, expecting some silly "Aussie bloke" punchline straight out of an old Castlemaine XXXX TV commercial.

"Nope. Heard it on the radio. The boy was sitting right beside the beer, which had the seat belt around it. The silly bastard had his priorities right, didn't he?"

I later discovered that it was a true story. The motorist was pulled over in his Holden Commodore on the Ross Highway, just south of Alice Springs. The child was sitting in the centre of the vehicle, unrestrained, beside the slab of VB beer. According to a police officer at the scene, the driver "just looked at me blankly". One suspects the driver looks at a lot of people blankly. He was fined $750 for driving an unregistered and uninsured vehicle and, let us not forget, for failing to restrain a child with a seat belt.

Parental licences are coming. It is only a matter of time.

Monday, 19 May

38 weeks today. I asked to be given a guided tour of my wife's hospital bag this evening. Organised to a fault, she packed the bag a couple of weeks ago. The hospital bag is self-explanatory, containing the essentials for mother and child during the birthing process and the subsequent days in the hospital.

Nursing bras for breastfeeding (hopefully); breast pads; sanitary pads; toiletries; nightgown, dressing gown and slippers; 30 disposable nappies; baby clothes and baby mittens (to minimise facial scratching) are the fundamental contents for any hospital bag and ours is zipped up and ready to go.

My job is to do the cameras, the phones and the "Push It Real Good" baby CD.

Saturday, 24 May

I was a little abrupt with my old mum this evening. As we chatted online, she made a fairly innocuous comment about the birth and I overreacted. In my defence, my irritation was not directed at my mother, but someone was going to cop it eventually. And unfortunately, that person turned out to be her.

People usually want to help, but they do have a peculiar way of showing it. If someone is about to have his tonsils out, I would remark positively that when I had a tonsillectomy, the surgery was routine with little discomfort. It would be grossly inconsiderate of me to claim that the doctor dropped one of the tonsils down my throat and I have not been able to swallow baked beans since. That of course never happened. But if it had, what would either of us gain from me sharing that story? Do you see where I am going with this?

As we move into the final days, hopefully, of the pregnancy, the gory stories are piling up with depressing consistency. My sister sent me a touching email, recalling all the trials and tribulations of her first birth. She said that all the pain and suffering will be forgotten when the baby is handed to us and I believe her. She also told us to expect the worst. I understand the logic. Expect the worst and the labour can neither shock nor disappoint. But I want to expect the best. I'm already shitting myself about parenthood. I see little value in fretting over things that may not happen and situations that I cannot control even if they do come to pass.

But the word "worst" is an extremely popular one at the moment.

"Do you want to know what the worst thing about pregnancy is?" a friend asked earlier this week.

No, of course I don't want to know, I thought. I'd rather batter myself over the head with this computer keyboard but that would be a futile exercise because your gleeful smile says you're going to share your dispiriting anecdote anyway.

"Yeah, sure, why not?" I muttered meekly.

"The worst thing about a pregnancy is when you are overdue by more than a week," she said. "The baby literally comes out overcooked, all red and blotchy, almost crispy."

A grotesque image of a newborn baby spinning around in a microwave oven popped into my head involuntarily and I was unable to get rid of it. I was not a happy camper.

"Ah, yeah, that's right," interjected another friend, who had just caught the tail end of the conversation and was eager to contribute to the top ten list of the worst things about pregnancy.

"I knew a guy whose wife had the same problem. She went past her due date and she began to look like she was overcooked, too. She was wrinkled and started to break out in sores."

"It's funny, when you think about it," I mumbled, adding a smile to take the edge of what I was about to say. "People always want to tell you the worst things about pregnancy, don't they? They never want to talk about the best things."

My confused friends stared at me, clearly wondering if it was medication time.

Life will never be the same again. That's the other one. Life will never be the same again. Without slipping into unnecessary hyperbole, people share this nugget of blindingly obvious wisdom at least once a day. Should we survive the ceaseless, ghastly terror that is the baby's delivery, we are in for a devastating bombshell. Life will never be the same again. Someone mentioned this to me yesterday—he wasn't the only person to say it in that hour—and nodded thoughtfully, clearly believing he had just quoted Voltaire.

I had never thought of that, mate. What I had planned to do was stick the baby in a cupboard drawer and go back to watching the football.

I have been recommended ... no, ordered, in some cases

... to sleep now because—and this may come as something of a surprise—babies sleep fitfully and inconsistently and often demand to be fed throughout the night. I have been told to go to the cinema, the theatre, a restaurant, a football match, the outback and the toilet because I will never be able to do so again. Things can only get worse. It's life, Jim, but not as we know it. That's not a quote from *Star Trek*. That's a comment on fatherhood.

I am refusing to buy into the cynicism. Yes, I know. When I become a parent, I will understand. That old parenthood chestnut is proving popular, too. When I've got a screaming kid in one ear, my wife in the other and I'm knee deep in nappies; the bills are piling up; the sink is full of dishes and I have not slept for 27 years, I will change my tune. Naïve optimism will be destroyed and I will step over to the cynical dark side.

My mother is not particularly cynical. She sends text messages every day, enquiring about my wife's well-being as the due date draws closer. That is what excitable grandparents-to-be do. But tonight as we chatted online, her opening suggestions gradually gave way to the more familiar, scaremongering comments that I had been growing tired of lately. Make sure the doctors and midwives do not carry out any procedures without our consent (we have already discussed this with Dr Derek); insist that our birth plan is strictly followed (ditto); when the baby is born, make sure the midwives do not take it away without our consent (that would be against our hospital's policy) and on the lecture went.

The outcome was inevitable. I took a good month's worth of suppressed frustration and unleashed it on my unsuspecting mother.

"Mum, we've been getting these kind of comments for weeks,"

I said. "If we're not being told our lives will never be the same, we're being told to expect the worst in pregnancy and hearing all these horror stories that happen at the end of the third trimester. We're having a baby, mum. We're not being executed."

There was a brief, uncomfortable silence.

"You've got to see it from our point of view," my mum finally replied. "We're all on the other side of the planet. My son is having his first baby in a foreign country, using a health system we know nothing about. We all hate the idea of you being alone. That's why we're all worried over here."

I felt like a shit for the rest of the evening.

Sunday, 25 May

My mother sent me a text message today that read: "You are both ready for whatever happens now."

"We'll do the best we can," I replied. "And we do appreciate you encouraging us every day."

That's all we had to say.

Wednesday, 28 May

I spent an entertaining evening drawing on my wife's back with a blue permanent marker. I had to ink over four fading rectangles on her lower back, two on either side of her spine. When the time comes, I will place electrode pads over the rectangles and send electrical pulses into my wife. I am not allowed to shout "clear" when I do it.

Like many parents-to-be, we would prefer a natural birth, if it is medically possible. But if we can introduce any devices that may prevent my wife from being in so much pain that she rips the skin off my face, so much the better. She settled on a Transcutaneous Electrical Nerve Stimulator, or a TENS unit. The compact, clever little contraption produces electrical signals that are used to stimulate nerves through unbroken skin. The four pads are placed over the nerves that supply the womb. The tiny impulses of electric current then stimulate the body's natural pain relief system. Using a switch box, my wife can send a tingling sensation into her lower back each time she has a contraction and, hopefully, lessen the pain. I say hopefully because there are a number of obstetricians who maintain that the TENS machine is ineffective. There is a risk that if the strength, frequency or length of the electric current is turned up too high, the overstimulation may intensify the pain. Most pregnancy books acknowledge that the TENS machine can provide some relief but may offer little comfort during a particularly painful contraction. We can only wait and see.

My wife picked up a TENS machine from a local physiotherapy clinic earlier in the week. The physiotherapist advised her, in all seriousness, not to use the TENS machine while in the shower. If there are pregnant women out there contemplating a quick shower with an electronic device for company, then you might want to consider adoption.

My sister had previously mentioned that she had hired a TENS machine during her first pregnancy and that served as something of an endorsement to us. If the TENS machine was good enough for her …

However, she neglected to tell us about her experience with the electrical device until this evening when she decided it was in our interests for her to come clean.

"Make sure you attach those electrode pads properly," she warned. "They can come off if there's too much movement."

"I'll do my best," I said.

"Yeah, because I went to the toilet during labour with my TENS machine still attached. When I sat down, the whole lot fell into the toilet bowl."

"Bloody hell! Really?"

"Yeah, the pain was pretty bad but I didn't put the machine back on in case I electrocuted myself."

Thursday, 29 May

Dr Derek wanted in on our bet today. The midwife, who had originally predicted 30 May as the due date, conceded that the baby was unlikely to introduce itself within the next 24 hours so new bets were taken. I came up with the postnatal prize—the quintessentially English tea and cakes—and there are now four contestants. The midwife revised her bet to 1 June, my wife has knocked a couple of days off her original guess and has settled on 9 June, my tea and cakes is on 2 June and Dr Derek relied on insider information.

"Am I allowed to cheat?" he asked.

Before we had a chance to answer, he began probing my wife's tummy, pushing his fingers in gently around the cervix to locate the baby's head. When he found it, he closed his eyes and made circles with his fingers, seemingly circumnavigating the little one's head. Perhaps a seasoned obstetrician really does eventually feel the hand of Nostradamus on his shoulder, or maybe he was just playing to the audience. He nodded and opened his eyes.

"7 June," he said decisively.

I wish I could say my gut reaction was "Hey, that's just a week away." What I really thought was "Oh no, 7 June is the opening fixture of the Euro 2008 football championships" and

I immediately felt guilty. Such a response was uncalled for and unnecessary. I can record all the matches.

Sunday, 1 June

My mother called to tell us that we will definitely be having a June baby now, an obvious fact that both of us had overlooked. My son or daughter will be born this month. I am about to realise the only ambition I have consistently harboured since I was a child. Well, there were two long-standing ambitions, but unless I am suddenly offered a contract by West Ham United and score the winning goal in next year's FA Cup Final, fatherhood will win.

Monday, 2 June

40 weeks today. Our baby is the size of … a newborn baby! Today marks the end of the third trimester. We are approaching the finish line and ready to breast the tape. We've reached "Go" and are waiting patiently to collect $200 from Mother Nature. The nursery is decorated; the wardrobe is full of reasonably neutral baby clothes; the pantry is stocked with food for the self-sufficient, first-time parents; the baby's car seat is secure; the petrol tank is full; the baby's head should now be in proportion to its body; its eyes are open; the genitals are formed; and the testes are in the scrotum if it's a boy, which is always important. My unflappable wife is a picture of maternal radiance and I am running around in circles like a fly with one wing. Bring on the baby.

Parental instincts are kicking in and biological programming is reconfiguring my emotions towards parenthood. I feel prepared for parenthood. I am ready to be a daddy to my child. I want to be a father today, right now, at this very moment. Nothing else is important. Be my baby now.

Tuesday, 3 June

Naturally, we are still waiting. Fired up for fatherhood last night, I was overwhelmed with a euphoric sense of expectation which I am still struggling to control. My phlegmatic wife reminded me that babies are not generally born moments after passing the 40-week stage and suggested I pace myself. She was right. I will be dancing around the fringes of hysteria by the time we go to hospital if I do not curb my enthusiasm in the next few days.

I smiled at my wife. I am so in awe of this woman.

"What? What is it?" she asked.

"You will give birth any day now," I said. "How are you staying so calm?"

"There's not much I can do now, is there? Just rest and wait."

"Yeah, I suppose so."

What an amazing woman, I thought. I am truly lucky.

"Oh, by the way," she said. "2 June has been and gone. You lost your bet."

Suddenly, I didn't feel so lucky.

Wednesday, 4 June

D-Day. Due date. Baby day. The day that we introduce a human being into the world. The day that we hold our first child. This is the day that I have been waiting for since two lines popped up in that plastic contraption on 5 October. Did our baby arrive? Of course it didn't, and the anticlimactic feeling is unshakeable. We already knew that very few babies are born on their actual due date, but it still feels as though Christmas has been cancelled. We had Christmas Eve last night, giggling childishly as we tried to guess what might be left in our stocking (boy or girl). Unable to sleep because of a heightened state of apprehension, we watched *Billy Elliot* (its working-class father-son relationship makes me blubber every time) to get us in the festive mood and rounded off the night by saying how proud we would be as parents if our child made it into the Royal Ballet School.

We woke up to find that our stocking was still empty. This is perfectly normal. Only 5 per cent of women deliver on their estimated due dates. But I had always suspected that the baby would come early. Perhaps my hunch was a combination of wishful thinking, impatience and my irritatingly tidy mind. The home is ready, our bags are packed and I have cleared my schedule, so come on, child, be like your father and fit snugly into *his* prearranged timetable.

Our baby did not oblige, surprisingly enough, but it was not for the want of trying on our part. My wife had a sudden, unexpected surge of energy today and found it difficult to remain still for more than a few minutes at a time. So we took a symbolic drive to the beach at Point Addis, one of our top Australian locations and an early contender for our baby's name. As we snaked our way through the forest's winding road towards the ocean, we hit a number of potholes on the bumpy surface.

"Well, you know what they say," I said to my wife as we bounced our way to Point Addis. "If you want to trigger the labour process, drive over a rugged road."

"Wait. Stop the car," she replied, suddenly clutching her tummy with both hands.

"What? What is it?" I said, executing an emergency stop in the middle of the deserted road.

"Look," my wife exclaimed. "There's a load of kangaroos grazing over there."

I almost bloody left her there.

Thursday, 5 June

At 10.45 a.m., we turned up for the weekly appointment with the midwife that I hadn't wanted to keep. When our midwife originally booked this particular appointment several weeks ago, I laughed theatrically and insisted that such a booking would prove redundant. Our baby will be punctual, I stated confidently. Well, it wasn't. Not surprisingly, the routine check-up had a perfunctory, lacklustre feel about it. Neither my wife nor I wanted to be there. We wanted to be in the nearby hospital cradling our firstborn. Once the due date passes, the impatience never leaves you.

My wife's weight and blood pressure were satisfactory as were the baby's approximate size and heart rate. There was not much else to do. Even the midwife was stuck for something to say.

"So, er, what should we do now?" I asked.

"Nothing really," replied the midwife. "Babies are very rarely born before the due date, particularly firstborns."

This may be true, but it is of no comfort.

"How far should we go before we have to make any sort of decision?" my wife piped up.

"Oh, some hospitals will let you go up to two weeks before inducing you. We prefer not to wait quite that long, but the decision is entirely yours."

"I don't know," my wife said.

We really didn't know. How could we make such a decision? How are first-time parents expected to know when the appropriate moment is to step in and give Nature a shove?

After much discussion between my wife and me, we settled on next Thursday as the date to go into hospital to consider inducing the labour. It is a week from today and the baby would be eight days overdue by then so it seemed as good a date as any.

"See you on Saturday," Dr Derek shouted from the hallway. Saturday is Dr Derek's bet. The man's professionalism knows no bounds.

"Seriously, though, if I do not see you on Saturday, then maybe we'll meet again next Thursday at the hospital."

I sincerely hope not. I am still banking on Nature determining our baby's birthday rather than Dr Derek.

Friday, 6 June

I realise now that we are not alone. Most doctors consider a full-term pregnancy to range from 38 to 42 weeks. When the midwife made the comment yesterday, we were shocked. We knew overdue babies were common, but 42 weeks? The thought of waiting another fortnight seems preposterous. Perhaps that demonstrates my ignorance or perhaps it shows that no one had highlighted 42-week pregnancies before. Every pregnancy book that we have consulted in the past six months pretty much wraps things up with a blue or pink bow just after 40 weeks. No doctor, obstetrician or midwife ever raised the figure 42. If they had, we might not be so apprehensive now. Only after I read up on prolonged pregnancies did I realise that anything up to 42 weeks is not a cause for concern. According to the American College of Obstetricians and Gynecologists, for instance, 10 per cent of all pregnancies go past 42 weeks. That's a huge number of late babies when you think about it. Why are expectant parents not given this information sooner? We could have used it in the past few days.

Naturally, there are 101 things to do when you are overdue to try and bring on labour, according to the books. The activities include walking, aerobics, yoga, shopping, listening to music, going to the movies, watching a favourite TV show, eating spicy food and indulging in a therapeutic massage. And then there's the most obvious and delicate one, the one that will work up a sweat, certainly, but may not be altogether flattering.

"You two need to get your leg over," my mother-in-law pointed out this evening on the phone.

"What? You can't say that, mum," replied her incredulous daughter.

"There's nothing wrong with it. Sex is what you need. It'll push that baby right out."

"Mum, please, we're not going to talk about this now."

"What? It's natural. It's a natural thing. I saw it on that programme."

"Which programme? A nature programme?"

"No, the one where Rachel and Ross try to have sex to get the baby out."

"You mean *Friends*? We're not Rachel and Ross, mum."

"Tell me about it."

The main problem with going past the due date, apart from my mother-in-law, is the nagging doubt. What if the date of 4 June was incorrectly assigned? Pinpointing the precise age of a foetus is hardly an exact science. Calculations can be based on a variety of methods, including the last menstrual period, the size of the uterus, foetal movement and heartbeat and, of course, the first ultrasound scan. Every method has considerable margin for error. If the menstrual history is inaccurate, then the methodology is flawed from the outset. Basically, our baby could be younger than we think. Our original due date was 14 June and my wife is still being castigated for being too small. Perhaps the initial prediction was more accurate than the current date. Either way, the uncertainty must drive first-time parents crazy. It is certainly not doing us any favours.

Clearly, I needed a second opinion. I called my mother.

"Mum, I know I was a fair size when I was born," I said. "Was I overdue?"

"No, mate, you were two days early."

"Oh, was I? Yeah, that's right. I remember now."

My voice trailed off, making no effort to hide the disappointment.

"Don't worry about it," my mum reassured. "This baby will pop out any day now, I know it will. And anyway, you know what you can do."

"What's that?"

"Have sex."

Saturday, 7 June

We had to get out of the house. When first-time parents go past their due date, they are not scintillating company. In addition, they cannot sit still for very long without looking at a clock or calendar. We decided to go for a walk by the Barwon River as we thought that the exercise may encourage the baby to wriggle its way south. We also thought that the change of scenery might stop us from going stir-crazy.

The trip ended in the hospital.

"Here, I haven't felt any movements since this morning," my wife said, rubbing her tummy, as we strolled past some gum trees.

"Really, that's it. This is it. This is it," I shouted, while performing an unexpected jig down the footpath. "You're going into labour. This is it."

"No, it's probably nothing. But the hospital's antenatal card told us to call them if the foetal movement slowed down."

I was already dialling. Within the hour, we were on our way to the hospital as the staff asked us to go for a routine heartbeat test.

"Put the camera on. Put the camera on," I repeated excitedly as I drove my silent wife to the hospital. "We've got to record every stage of the birth. Put the camera on while I'm driving."

"No," my wife said quietly.

"No? What's wrong with you? This could be it."

"But what if it's not," she whispered, staring down at her tummy. "What if it's something else? The baby hasn't moved for hours, Neil."

I stopped talking. I was not particularly worried, but my wife clearly was so we drove for the next few minutes in silence. It was not yet 7 p.m., but the dark, damp wintry streets were deserted. There were street parties going on inside my head, but all was quiet in the real world. The contrast was eerie.

Just as we turned in towards the hospital car park, my wife stiffened and grabbed my left arm.

"What's wrong? What's happened?" I asked.

My wife smiled.

"The baby just kicked and it's still kicking."

"The cheeky little sod."

This impudent baby of ours wasn't going anywhere this evening. We should have called the hospital and told the midwives that our giggling foetus was playing its first game of hide-and-seek. But we were almost there and what's a little white lie if it gives us the chance to meet the midwives and poke around the maternity ward for a bit?

A smiley midwife wrapped two clamps at either end of the uterus and told my wife to lie back for a while. The top clamp measured contractions and the other one the baby's heartbeat. She switched the machine on and the baby's rapid heartbeat exploded around the room. My instinctive reaction surprised me. I was extremely relieved. Perhaps I had been more concerned than I had let on.

"Doesn't that sound great?" the midwife asked.

It really did.

"Everything looks fine to me," she continued. "We'll just monitor the heartbeat's fluctuations and then you can go home. We'll see you again in the next few days, I'm sure."

I could feel that impatience taking hold again.

"Well, seeing as we're here, is there any chance that we might squeeze the baby out now?" I asked the midwife. "It seems a shame to waste the trip."

The midwife laughed. She thought I was joking. I think I was.

Sunday, 8 June

Every TV channel we switched to this evening seemed to be airing a newborn being squeezed out of a vagina. Australia's popular current affairs programme, *60 Minutes*, opened tonight's show with a debate on natural vs Caesarean births. I kid you not. The TV struggled with the countless images of beaming mothers cradling their babies. My wife was not amused.

Emotionally, we are stranded in no man's land. We are geared up for the final push psychologically, only for it to be unexpectedly delayed. Like all inexperienced, uncertain first-time parents, we want to know that we are not alone. So we read to seek reassurance. Doing so only adds to the uncertainty, however. According to the World Health Organization and International Federation of Gynecology and Obstetrics guidelines, a prolonged pregnancy is a gestational age of 42 weeks or more (greater than 294 days). We are at 41 weeks. Give it another week or so and the perinatal mortality rate (stillbirths plus early neonatal deaths) rises to 4 to 7 per 1,000 births. This is double the rate for 40-week deliveries. Then there is the placenta. With every passing day, more calcium is deposited into the placenta, which may lead to its calcification. This, in turn, will reduce its function. Other risks include umbilical cord compression, the baby inhaling its own poop and postnatal complications like seizures and hypoglycaemia. Our family already knows enough about the dangers of hypoglycaemia.

Oh, and the baby keeps growing. Generally speaking, post-term babies are bigger than those born on or close to term. My wife is tiny and remains so. When we went for our first routine check-up on 1 November, our local GP mentioned her petite pelvis. That nagging fear has been chipping away since 4 June. It is the only concern that I do not share with my wife.

Monday, 9 June

41 weeks today. The week that is irresponsibly not included in any of the pregnancy books that we have consulted has begun. Today marks my wife's prediction. When she originally piped up with 9 June, both the midwife and I laughed dismissively. My wife's diminutive frame indicated that the baby was running out of room. She might be the one carrying our child, but she had to be way off. The pregnancy would never go this far ...

At 11.30 a.m., she woke up with an aching, persistent, period-like pain around her belly button but thought little of it. She had suffered discomfort for several days now in her upper and lower back, so this new development did not feel particularly ominous. Pain is pain.

"Neil, come here," she called out from the bathroom.

I wandered over and opened the door.

"Bloody hell," I shouted, throwing my hand up to my nose and recoiling violently as though I had been smashed in the face with a poo bat.

"Do you think it's smelly?" my wife asked nervously.

"Smelly? I think my nose just melted."

"This could be it then, I think."

"This could be what?"

"This could be *it.*"

She looked up at me slowly, her face a confusing mix of excitement and anxiety.

"The pains are more consistent. I think they started when I was still asleep," she said. "And the books say that it's common to have a really smelly poo as labour starts."

"Well, they don't come any smellier than that, mate."

We both looked at each other and smiled. We didn't say anything. We just stared at each other. Eventually, I crouched down and hugged my wife briefly, thinking only of our firstborn rather than the dreadful stench that was choking the toilet bowl.

Then I stood up, caressed her cheek slowly, took a deep breath and panicked.

"Right, we need to get your hospital bag into the car, stick the TENS machine on your back, call the hospital to let them know you're on the way and move the car round to the front of the house. Right, I'll get the hospital bag," I bellowed, running off down the hallway.

"Neil," my wife shouted. "Come back here."

I dashed back to the bathroom.

"What? What is it now?" I asked quickly, my eyes darting all over her body looking for any new symptoms.

"If it is labour, it's only just started," she whispered slowly. "It could be hours before I even go to hospital."

"Really? Oh, I'll go and watch the rest of the Germany and Poland match then."

I didn't really. I ran her a warm bath, eased her in slowly, handed over the latest Jodi Picoult novel and left her in peace for a couple of hours.

As a first labour can exceed fourteen hours, it is recommended that the first few hours are spent at home. When mothers recount horrifying tales of protracted pain and being stuck in a hospital bed for twenty hours, some are the result of being admitted into hospital far too early. Midwives cannot speed up labour (unless a medical complication compels them to). They can only pop in occasionally and check the baby's heartbeat and the mother's blood pressure. That's why they prefer the labouring mother to stay at home for as long as possible. Yes, it may save critical bed space, but it is also better for the woman to remain in a familiar environment for as long as possible.

The logic is sound, but I dispensed with logic just after my wife dropped a putrid depth charge into our toilet bowl. Waiting for the contractions to gain momentum was excruciating (it was hardly a walk in the park for my wife) and a sense of uselessness took hold. I could neither take the pain away nor accelerate the labour. I had to do something. I made my wife lunch, cleaned up the kitchen, wiped down every surface in the house, swept all the tiled floors, tidied up the bassinet and the nursery, took out the rubbish and moved the car into position. Then my wife intervened.

"Neil, stop that housework and get in here," she hissed.

I ran into the living room. My wife was on all fours on the living room floor, leaning on the sofa and swaying from side to side.

"Get the TENS machine," she whispered. With her head pressed forward against the sofa cushion, she was barely audible. "The pain's getting really bad now."

Kneeling behind my wife, who was still on all fours, I threw her nightgown over her shoulders and rubbed her back gently.

"Seeing as I'm here, any chance of a quick ..."

"Get on with it."

But she chuckled in spite of herself. That was good enough for me.

I stuck the four electrode pads on her upper and lower back. I handed my wife the surge button, which she was to press and hold down throughout each contraction, and I connected the electrodes' wires to the control box. There were two counters: one for frequency, the other for amplitude. I turned the frequency to ten and then switched the amplitude dial all the way round too. My wife's body shook.

"What the fuck did you just do?" she screamed.

"I turned the amplitude thing round, like the frequency."

"You only increase that as the contraction pains increase. About three or four should be enough of a surge at this stage. How far did you turn it?"

"Round to ten."

"Bloody hell, Neil. Are you trying to kill us both?"

My wife took charge of the TENS device.

I was tasked with phoning the hospital.

"Hello, my name is Neil Humphreys and I'm having a baby," I blurted out. "What time do you want us?"

"Well, this is actually the receptionist. I'll put you through to the birthing suite."

"OK, thank you … They're putting me through to the birthing suite," I called out to my groaning wife.

"Oh, hi. My wife is in labour, I think, and we were wondering what time we should come in."

"Sure, that's fine," replied an authoritative, but warm, voice that had clearly been on the other end of this call a thousand times before. "What's happened so far?"

"Well, she woke up at 11.30 a.m. with period-type pains. She's had a bath and now the pains are more frequent, around every six or seven minutes. We've got a TENS machine, and that's helping a bit, but the pain is increasing now and …

"OK, that all sounds normal to me. Has she had a vaginal swab?"

"Er, not today, no."

I heard a stifled giggle.

"No, what I mean is has she already had a vaginal swab?"

"Oh, I see, right. Yes she has. Yes."

"Right, well, everything sounds really good. If your wife is comfortable at home with the TENS machine, you should hang on there for a bit longer."

"So you think this is it, then?" I asked excitedly. "This is not a false alarm or a false start?"

"No, it sounds like your baby is definitely on its way."

I put the phone down and danced out of the office and into the living room.

"The baby's on its way. The baby's on its way," I shouted,

pirouetting around the living room like Fred Astaire. "Did you hear that? Our baby is on its way!"

I looked down at my oblivious wife. Still on all fours, she was rocking from side to side. Her fists clenched the sides of the sofa and her head was buried in the cushion. Her tears had formed a damp patch on the cushion. I knelt down beside her, rested my head on the cushion beside hers and gently tilted her head back so our noses touched. I had never seen her so vulnerable before.

"The pain is too much," she whispered. "I don't know if I can do this anymore."

"Right, that's it," I asserted. "We're leaving right now."

It was my turn to be decisive.

At 8 p.m., I ushered my wincing wife into the car and then ran back to lock the front door. At that moment, our next door neighbours appeared on their doorstep.

"Woo hoo," they cried. "Are you off to the hospital? Is this it?"

"Yep, I think so," I shouted back quickly. "Got to hurry now."

"Is there anything we can do?" they continued.

"Nope, we're fine really. Speak soon."

I jumped into my wife's car and attempted to reverse out onto the street. My groaning wife was sitting in the back, with her head between her legs, looking every bit the drunk sitting on the kerb in the early hours. Our neighbours continued to wave at us from their doorstep and shouted kind words of encouragement. Meanwhile I was demonstrating my inability to reverse in a straight line. The first attempt almost hit a fence and the second squashed several plants. In the rear view mirror, I could see both my wife rocking backwards and forwards in pain and the neighbours laughing at my haphazard attempts to reach the street. When my third attempt almost removed a gate, my wife snapped.

"Shall I fucking drive?" she croaked.

With ego sufficiently pricked, I took a deep breath, straightened the car and backed out onto the street, still only missing the fence by a matter of centimetres. She had two contractions during the short journey. By the time she had another one, moments after I pulled up in front of the hospital entrance, she could barely stand. A kindly, middle-aged midwife guided us into the birthing suite and my wife flopped onto the bed. She could not lie still. Rolling from side to side, no position offered any respite from the incessant and increasing pain. The midwife checked the baby's heartbeat, which was slowing down, as expected at this stage. My wife, on the other hand, was in some distress. The midwife attempted to take her blood pressure but my wife almost swatted her aside as she continued to wriggle around the bed.

"I can't do this, Neil," she groaned. She was now crying openly, struggling to cope with the pain and a growing sense that an entirely natural birth was unlikely to happen.

"The TENS machine isn't working anymore. And I'm not going to be able to take the pain."

I held her hand, stroked her face and assured her that I would not allow her to suffer for much longer. At least she seemed convinced.

"Is there nothing we can do for my wife?" I asked the midwife, who was already busying herself at the side of the bed.

"I'm just hooking up the nitrous oxide now," she said optimistically.

Ah, the gas and air. That will do the trick. I had seen the movies and TV sitcoms that had the outrageously painful labour scenes followed by all involved getting high on the gas and air.

As I held my breath, my wife took a couple of deep breaths of nitrous oxide and promptly retched. Her face turned a lovely lime green as she battled to keep her lunch down. Gas and air promptly joined the TENS machine on the scrap heap. My sickly wife was almost delirious and we were running out of ideas. If this was the first stage of labour, she would not make it to the second.

I guessed my wife's deteriorating condition was serious when she threatened to shove the foetal stethoscope up the midwife's arse. As a rule, she is unfailingly polite. However, as she moved steadily from the first stage of labour (the womb muscles contract to open up the cervix) to the transition stage (the contractions are more frequent, almost every minute, and more sustained), my wife left the building. The pain transformed her, replacing her with a distant, volatile zombie. Watching such a shocking metamorphosis take hold of the woman I had loved for almost half my life and knowing I was utterly powerless to prevent it from happening was easily the worst part of the labour process. I did manage to stop her from decking the midwife though.

Having discarded every other pain relief contraption in the birthing suite (bed, pillows, sofa and stool), we tried the Swiss exercise ball. My wife wrapped herself over the top of the ball and rolled slowly from side to side. The therapeutic benefits were already proving negligible when the midwife came over with her foetal stethoscope. The unflappable woman gamely attempted to locate our firstborn's heartbeat as my wife stubbornly refused to stop rolling on her giant rubber ball.

"I'm just going to sneak in and check on baby," the midwife said breezily. Midwives always say "baby", rather than "the baby", as if that is the child's intended name in honour of the girl in *Dirty Dancing* who was put in the corner.

"So we just need to roll this way slightly so we can check baby's heart," the midwife continued, overlooking the rather obvious fact that my panting partner had ignored her request.

My wife pulled me close to her face and whispered into my ear.

"Make that woman go away," she muttered. "Otherwise, I will stick that fucking stethoscope up her arse."

"Maybe we should get my wife settled back on the bed and then we can measure the heartbeat," I suggested diplomatically.

The midwife smiled and nodded. It was water off a duck's back.

By 9.30 p.m., we needed to make a decision quickly. My wife staggered over to the toilet and, even with my assistance, lacked both the physical strength and the mental resolve to make it back to the bed. I practically held her up as she washed her hands. At that point, Dr Derek sauntered into the room, looking every inch the cool and composed obstetrician. He put a reassuring hand on my wife's shoulder, gazed into her eyes and smiled encouragingly.

"Is there anything I can do to help?" he asked.

She ignored him. She simply ignored him. It was extraordinary. I had never seen her ignore anyone before. A drunken Australian tourist once tried to put his hand up her skirt in a Singaporean bar and she still refused to dignify his actions with silence. She told him where to go instead. Yet here she was, waddling past the considerate man who had nurtured her through six months of the pregnancy. Superficially, her actions smacked of remarkable rudeness, but it was more than that. She did not see him. He did not exist. The pain had consumed my wife and she was now in a trancelike state. She was present in the room, but she was not there.

With teeth-clenching willpower that took the breath away and broke the heart, my weeping wife clambered up onto the bed for Dr Derek to examine her.

"That's just wonderful," he said calmly to my wife, as she wriggled around the bed. "You're already more than 5 cm dilated."

She was too distraught to answer.

"So we're halfway there, doc," I said. "How much longer?"

"I would say at least four or five hours."

My wife tried to sit up suddenly but fell back onto the pillows. She grabbed my hand.

"I can't do it, Neil," she said, crying. "I can't do it. I'm sorry. I can't take this pain for another four hours. Promise me you'll make the pain go away."

I held her hand tightly, forced a smile and nodded before looking away. Big boys do cry, but they cannot cry when their wives need them most. My wife's anxieties were already overwhelming. She did not need mine, not now. My tears could be saved for later.

"OK, doc, my wife's pain relief is my only concern now," I said decisively. "What are our options?"

With time clearly not on my wife's side, Dr Derek broke it down quickly. Nitrous oxide made my wife nauseous and repeated exposure would not overcome that while pethidine's effectiveness was not much different to the TENS machine. My wife had already cranked the amplitude up to ten, sending the most intense surges possible into her back and they were now doing nothing to ease the discomfort. Dr Derek confirmed what we already knew. The only way up was the needle down in the spine.

Things moved quickly after that. Midwives and doctors came and went with such rapidity that proceedings took on a dreamlike quality. Dr Derek left the room to make the call to the anaesthetist. The midwives prepared my wife for the epidural, moving her from one side to the other to check her blood pressure and examine her back as she appeared to drift in and out of consciousness. Her face permanently screwed up in agony, she was poked and prodded around but she barely noticed. At one point, she was moved onto her side and her gown rode up her legs, exposing her backside to all in the room. Then she flopped onto her back, her nightgown still above her waist, revealing her private parts. I gently and discreetly pulled the gown back down again to protect her modesty. I was not being naïve. I knew that in a few hours, almost everyone present in the room would be opening up her vagina to facilitate our baby's birth, but there was a time and a place. She reminded me of those old women in care facilities whose modesty had been stripped away by illness or infirmity. The pain had usurped her dignity and she was past caring.

The anaesthetist suddenly appeared in the birthing suite. I say suddenly because he was an exceptionally short man and easy to miss. We shook hands quickly and introduced ourselves. He was delighted to hear that his latest epidural patient was British.

"I love England," he declared, as he donned a pair of surgical gloves and sized up his collection of needles. "It's the heritage about the place I love. Australia's great, but it doesn't have the sense of history or those great historic castles."

Clearly, the relaxed anaesthetist had performed this operation hundreds of times before and that inspired confidence. But this was our first time and I really was in no mood to debate the cultural value of the Tower of London.

"Yeah, England's great," I said quickly. "My wife's in quite a bit of pain, here."

"Oh, we'll soon take care of that. Just a few more minutes and it'll all be over. Here, do you know something?"

"What's that?" I asked nervously.

"They have some wonderful documentaries about British history, don't they?"

"Yeah, they do. So does my wife need to lie still because the pain is making her move a lot and you're going to put that needle in her spine."

"No, she'll be fine. It's very straightforward … I'll tell you one British programme I really like—*Top Gear*. That Jeremy Clarkson and his cars. He's funny, isn't he?"

"Yes, I love the man. How much longer, doc?"

"Oh, I'd say we're just about ready."

My weakening wife grabbed my hand as the doctor moved her onto her side and told her to prepare for a small electric shock in her back. The needle was enormous and my wife was fidgeting tremendously, indicating to my non-medical mind that the margins for error had to be small.

"Look at me," I whispered, as I rested my head beside hers on the pillow. "Just keep looking at me. You must try and stay still, mate."

I was desperate for her not to move unnecessarily. I was also mindful of the foreboding size of the needle. I did not want her to see it.

"OK then, here we go," the bubbly anaesthetist said.

My wife's entire body jolted. Her back arched forwards as she let out a sudden high-pitched scream. She started shaking violently, then the mucus plug gave way, creating a little puddle of blood at the end of the bed. Next her waters broke. All within the space of 60 seconds. We wrapped my shivering wife in a couple of blankets. The midwife moved swiftly to clean up the blood and the amniotic fluid while the chirpy anaesthetist shook my hand and informed me that the operation had been a complete success. He then proudly pointed out that he had been trained at a British hospital so I could always say that my native land had been involved in the birth of my first child.

All in all, it was an eventful couple of minutes.

An hour later, my wife was sitting up in bed, making idiotic jokes and sipping a glass of orange juice. The anaesthetist's chatty self-assurance was certainly justified. The outcome was perfect. The nerves in my wife's lower back were numb but she could still detect the pressure of each contraction to enable her to push out the baby herself. This was important to her. She wanted to *feel* her baby coming out.

We now had a pair of wonderful midwives dedicated to our delivery and they checked in on us periodically to determine whether the cervix was fully dilated. My wife was struggling to stay awake when one of the midwives examined her again and nodded to herself.

"That's good," she said softly. "That's really good."

She looked up at my wife and smiled.

"It's time," she whispered.

They wanted to get me involved. I understand that now. When my wife started pushing, my contributions included stroking her hair and biting my bottom lip anxiously. Clearly, the father-to-be should have a more prominent role. The midwives had been holding my wife's legs and telling her to push along with the contractions when the midwife on her right beckoned me over.

"Why don't you hold this leg while I call Dr Derek?" she said.

"Yeah, sure, if you think I can do it," I replied excitedly.

"Of course you can," she asserted.

Of course I couldn't.

Moments later, after a particularly hefty push, I let go of my wife's leg to kiss her gently on the forehead, only to watch it flop spectacularly off the bed and swing limply over the side.

"Neil, my leg is numb from the epidural," my wife screamed. "If you want this baby, I suggest you go and pick up my leg and bring it back."

Suitably chastised, I retrieved my wife's leg and promised to hold on to it tightly.

Watching her push, I knew that she felt she had something to prove during the second stage. If the midwives asked for two sustained pushes, she gave three. If they called for three, she squeezed out four and sustained the pressure until her face and ears turned purple. I knew why she was doing it. The epidural had clearly been the correct decision, but she had fought against it until the pain had overwhelmed her. She accepted that the epidural was necessary, but she would not accommodate any other external help. Only she would push our baby out.

When Dr Derek arrived, the birth ventured into surreal territory. Every unique development was so natural and yet so alien, so obvious and yet so incomprehensible, that my brain struggled to compute what my eyes could see.

"Do you want to see your baby's head?" Dr Derek asked. Or at least I think that's what he said. How can I look down at my baby's head? I thought to myself. I drifted over to the bottom of the bed, struggling to breathe as the room swirled around me. Garbled words of encouragement echoed softly around the room as I peered cautiously between my wife's legs. I stared for several seconds, unable to comprehend the primeval image before me. "That's a head," said a distant voice inside my own head. "That's a tiny human head covered in matted, blond hair. How can that even be possible? It cannot be there."

"What can you see? What can you see?" a voice asked,

somewhere in the distance. "What can you see? Can you see anything?"

Overdosing on a natural high, I dreamily looked up at the purple, panting woman staring back at me. She obviously wanted something.

"Well, what did you see?"

"I saw our baby's head."

I heard the words come out, but I did not say them.

"What does it look like? What does our baby look like?"

"When I was a kid, I used to collect bags of tripe for our dog," I heard a voice say. "Well, it looks just like that. Our baby's head looks like a little plate of tripe."

Who was this person? It couldn't possibly be me rambling on about old pet dogs and tripe. A drunken, babbling, incoherent idiot had taken my place.

"And it also doesn't have ginger hair. That's great, isn't it? The baby doesn't have ginger hair. Woo hoo!"

Someone, please, tell this dickhead to shut up.

I was floating now, high above everyone else in the birthing suite. I was calmly disconnected from the hubbub and looking down upon proceedings. I saw myself reach forward and touch my baby's head. It was surprisingly soft and tender, like a damp sponge, and not at all hard or bony.

Dr Derek applied some lubricant around my wife's vaginal opening and it suddenly bulged as she put her head down and shuddered. Her entire body shook violently. The baby's head surged forward silently and a grey/blue, scrunched-up face flopped out of my wife and turned upwards. For a moment, I thought I had fathered a pug dog, but then its wrinkled, frowning face opened up dramatically, unmasking itself to reveal its eyes, nose and mouth. This human face flowered in front of me. Even the ears appeared to have been folded into three by an origami expert until they, too, opened to reveal themselves. The head now had a face staring back at me—my baby's face.

"Neil, Neil, quick! Come round here," I heard Dr Derek say, but I was dumbstruck. My feet had turned to clay and my eyes refused to move away from this tiny, hypnotic face.

"Neil, quick! The rest of your baby is about to come out," Dr Derek continued. "You can catch it yourself."

My baby was coming out. I was seconds away from holding my own baby. I found myself moving to the end of the bed, still staring at my baby's face. I felt Dr Derek grab my hands and place them in front of my baby's head. He was saying something about handling the baby, but he was inaudible. My subconscious had shut him out. He was extraneous, an irrelevance to the senses. Everything was locked in on the baby. Nothing else mattered now. Its shoulders, body and legs plopped out so quickly, the scene played out in slow motion. Dr Derek was still talking and gesturing with his hands but I couldn't hear him. I knew what to do. It was instinctive. I scooped up this fragile, wriggling little person and heard my mother's voice shout, "Safe heads, Neil. Safe hands. Don't drop it, boy." No chance. I've caught this one, mum. Covered in that white, slippery vernix, the baby almost did get away from me, but I held on. I will always hold on. I will never let go. Daddy's got safe hands.

I passed our baby to my beautiful wife and we giggled together. We haven't stopped giggling since. Dr Derek handed me a pair of scissors and asked me to cut the umbilical cord. I obliged without thinking. At that moment, I would have cut my own spinal cord without thinking. The midwife asked if she could take our baby over to the weighing machine when she suddenly stopped.

"Wait, there's something we need to do now," she said, handing our baby back to us. "You'd better have a look to see if you've got a boy or a girl."

Tuesday, 10 June 2008

At 4 a.m., I was left alone to cradle our sleeping baby for the first time. I had been a father for 44 minutes. My wonderful, precious wife was being helped by the two midwives to bathe her weary body, leaving me alone to gaze at our tiny creation. There were no tears, just an overwhelming sense of wonder and pride. I was 33 years old and already knew that I would never create something so perfect again. I kissed our baby gently on the cheek and reminded myself that this day had been inevitable. From the moment I understood what it meant to be a product of a broken home, I needed to be a father, a good father. I had a once-a-week dad. I just want to be a dad.

The late American anthropologist Margaret Mead once said that fathers are a biological necessity, but a social accident. Modern culture would support her theory, I suppose. For my sake, I hope she is wrong. In fact, my baby and I pledged to prove her wrong in the hospital. As we clung to each other in the deserted birthing suite, my baby suddenly woke up, stretched out an arm and waved it around frantically until it settled peacefully on my chest.

I was there. I will always be there for my beautiful, baby girl.

About the Author

In 1996, Neil Humphreys left Dagenham, England, to travel the world. The young Brit got as far as Toa Payoh, Singapore, and decided the rest of the world could wait.

By 2001, he was one of the country's best-selling authors. His first book, *Notes from an even Smaller Island*, became an immediate best-seller and travelled across Southeast Asia, Australia and Britain. BBC World said it was "a warts and all view of the city-state and celebrates many of the things most often criticised". In 2003, his second book, *Scribbles from the Same Island*, a compilation of his popular humour columns, also became a best-seller. In 2006, *Final Notes from a Great Island: A Farewell Tour of Singapore* completed the trilogy. The book went straight to No.1, making Humphreys one of Singapore's best-selling authors of the past decade.

Keen to explore an even bigger island, Humphreys now lives in Geelong, Australia. He writes for several magazines and newspapers in Singapore and Australia, and spends his weekends happily watching his girls go by.